D1543448

100 BEST
Chocolate
RECIPES

Publications International, Ltd.
Favorite Brand Name Recipes at www.fbnr.com

Pictured on the front cover: Easy Double Chocolate Chip Brownies *(page 46)*.

Pictured on the back cover *(clockwise from top left):* Jumbo 3-Chip Cookies *(page 6)*, Chocolate Intensity *(page 70)*, Lots o' Chocolate Bread *(page 143)* and Chocolate Peanut Butter Cups *(page 86)*.

ISBN-13: 978-1-4127-2425-8
ISBN-10: 1-4127-2425-2

Library of Congress Control Number: 2005910387

Manufactured in China.

8 7 6 5 4 3 2 1

Microwave Cooking: Microwave ovens vary in wattage. Use the cooking times as guidelines and check for doneness before adding more time.

Preparation/Cooking Times: Preparation times are based on the approximate amount of time required to assemble the recipe before cooking, baking, chilling or serving. These times include preparation steps such as measuring, chopping and mixing. The fact that some preparations and cooking can be done simultaneously is taken into account. Preparation of optional ingredients and serving suggestions is not included.

Contents

Chocolate-Packed Cookies 4

Brownies & Bars 34

Sinfully Rich Cakes 62

Decadent Desserts 86

Quick Chocolate Fixes 110

Chocolate for Breakfast 130

Acknowledgments 154

Index 155

Chocolate-Packed Cookies

Chocolate Gingersnaps

¾ **cup sugar**
1 **package (18¼ ounces) chocolate cake mix** *without* **pudding in the mix**
1 **tablespoon ground ginger**
2 **eggs**
⅓ **cup vegetable oil**

1. Preheat oven to 350°F. Spray cookie sheets with nonstick cooking spray.

2. Place sugar in shallow bowl. Combine cake mix and ginger in large bowl. Add eggs and oil; stir until well blended.

3. Shape dough into 1-inch balls, using about 1 tablespoon dough for each cookie. Roll in sugar to coat. Place 2 inches apart on prepared cookie sheets. Bake 10 minutes; remove to wire racks to cool completely.

Makes about 3 dozen cookies

*Clockwise from top left: Jumbo 3-Chip Cookies
(page 6), Chocolate Gingersnaps,
Milk Chocolate Florentine Cookies (page 20)
and Chocolate Almond Biscotti (page 12)*

Jumbo 3-Chip Cookies

4 cups all-purpose flour
1 teaspoon baking powder
1 teaspoon baking soda
1½ cups (3 sticks) butter, softened
1¼ cups granulated sugar
1¼ cups packed brown sugar
2 large eggs
1 tablespoon vanilla extract
1 cup (6 ounces) NESTLÉ® TOLL HOUSE® Milk Chocolate Morsels
1 cup (6 ounces) NESTLÉ® TOLL HOUSE® Semi-Sweet Chocolate Morsels
½ cup NESTLÉ® TOLL HOUSE® Premier White Morsels
1 cup chopped nuts

PREHEAT oven to 375°F.

COMBINE flour, baking powder and baking soda in medium bowl. Beat butter, granulated sugar and brown sugar in large mixer bowl until creamy. Beat in eggs and vanilla extract. Gradually beat in flour mixture. Stir in morsels and nuts. Drop dough by level ¼-cup measure 2 inches apart onto ungreased baking sheets.

BAKE for 12 to 14 minutes or until light golden brown. Cool on baking sheets for 2 minutes; remove to wire racks to cool completely.

Makes about 2 dozen cookies

Jumbo 3-Chip Cookies

Malted Milk Cookies

1 cup (2 sticks) butter, softened
¾ cup granulated sugar
¾ cup packed light brown sugar
1 teaspoon baking soda
2 eggs
2 squares (1 ounce each) unsweetened chocolate, melted and cooled
1 teaspoon vanilla
2¼ cups all-purpose flour
½ cup malted milk powder
1 cup chopped malted milk balls

1. Preheat oven to 375°F. Beat butter in large bowl with electric mixer at medium speed 30 seconds. Beat in sugars and baking soda. Add eggs, chocolate and vanilla; beat until well blended. Gradually beat in flour. Using spoon, stir in malted milk powder and malted milk balls.

2. Drop dough by rounded teaspoonfuls 2½ inches apart onto ungreased cookie sheets. Bake about 10 minutes or until edges are firm. Let cookies cool on cookie sheets 1 minute; remove to wire racks to cool completely.

Makes about 3 dozen cookies

Chocolate Peanut Butter Chip Cookies

8 (1-ounce) squares semi-sweet chocolate
3 tablespoons butter or margarine
1 (14-ounce) can EAGLE BRAND® Sweetened Condensed Milk
   (NOT evaporated milk)
2 cups biscuit baking mix
1 egg
1 teaspoon vanilla extract
1 cup (6 ounces) peanut butter-flavored chips

1. Preheat oven to 350°F. In large saucepan over low heat, melt chocolate and butter with EAGLE BRAND®; remove from heat. Add biscuit mix, egg and vanilla; with electric mixer, beat until smooth and well blended.

2. Let mixture cool to room temperature. Stir in peanut butter chips. Shape into 1¼-inch balls. Place 2 inches apart on ungreased baking sheets. Bake 6 to 8 minutes or until tops are lightly crusty. Cool. Store tightly covered at room temperature.

Makes about 4 dozen cookies

Malted Milk Cookies

Chocolate Crackletops

2 cups all-purpose flour
2 teaspoons baking powder
2 cups granulated sugar
½ cup (1 stick) butter or margarine
4 squares (1 ounce each) unsweetened baking chocolate, chopped
4 large eggs, lightly beaten
2 teaspoons vanilla extract
1¾ cups "M&M's"® Chocolate Mini Baking Bits
   Additional granulated sugar

Combine flour and baking powder; set aside. In 2-quart saucepan over medium heat, combine 2 cups sugar, butter and chocolate, stirring until butter and chocolate are melted; remove from heat. Gradually stir in eggs and vanilla. Stir in flour mixture until well blended. Chill mixture 1 hour. Stir in "M&M's"® Chocolate Mini Baking Bits; chill mixture an additional 1 hour.

Preheat oven to 350°F. Line cookie sheets with foil. With sugar-dusted hands, roll dough into 1-inch balls; roll balls in additional granulated sugar. Place about 2 inches apart onto prepared cookie sheets. Bake 10 to 12 minutes. Do not overbake. Cool completely on wire racks. Store in tightly covered container.   *Makes about 5 dozen cookies*

Chocolate Chip Macaroons

2½ cups flaked coconut
⅔ cup mini semisweet chocolate chips
⅔ cup sweetened condensed milk
1 teaspoon vanilla

1. Preheat oven to 350°F. Grease cookie sheets. Combine coconut, chocolate chips, milk and vanilla in medium bowl; mix until well blended.

2. Drop dough by rounded teaspoonfuls 2 inches apart onto prepared cookie sheets. Press dough gently with back of spoon to flatten slightly. Bake 10 to 12 minutes or until light golden brown. Let cookies cool on cookie sheets 1 minute; remove to wire racks to cool completely.
          Makes about 3½ dozen cookies

Chocolate Crackletops

Chocolate Almond Biscotti

**1 package DUNCAN HINES® Moist Deluxe® Dark Chocolate
  Cake Mix**
1 cup all-purpose flour
½ cup butter or margarine, melted
2 eggs
1 teaspoon almond extract
½ cup chopped almonds
  White chocolate, melted (optional)

1. Preheat oven to 350°F. Line 2 baking sheets with parchment paper.

2. Combine cake mix, flour, butter, eggs and almond extract in large bowl. Beat at low speed with electric mixer until well blended; stir in almonds. Divide dough in half. Shape each half into 12×2-inch log; place logs on prepared baking sheets. (Bake logs separately.)

3. Bake at 350°F for 30 to 35 minutes or until toothpick inserted in center comes out clean. Remove logs from oven; cool on baking sheets 15 minutes. Using serrated knife, cut logs into ½-inch slices. Arrange slices on baking sheets. Bake biscotti 10 minutes. Remove to cooling racks; cool completely.

4. Dip one end of each biscotti in melted white chocolate, if desired. Allow white chocolate to set at room temperature before storing biscotti in airtight container.　　　　　　　*Makes about 2½ dozen cookies*

Double Chocolate Oat Drops

MAZOLA NO STICK® Cooking Spray
2 cups (12 ounces) semisweet chocolate chips, divided
¼ cup (½ stick) margarine or butter
⅔ cup KARO® Light or Dark Corn Syrup
2 eggs
¼ teaspoon salt
4 cups uncooked quick oats
1 cup flaked coconut
1 cup coarsely chopped walnuts
⅔ cup packed brown sugar

1. Preheat oven to 350°F. Spray cookie sheets with cooking spray.

2. In medium heavy saucepan over low heat, combine 1 cup chocolate chips and margarine; stir just until melted. Remove from heat. Stir in corn syrup, eggs and salt.

3. In large bowl combine oats, coconut, walnuts and brown sugar. Add chocolate mixture; mix well. Stir in remaining 1 cup chocolate chips.

4. Drop by tablespoonfuls onto prepared cookie sheets. Bake 15 minutes (cookies will not change much in appearance during baking). Cool 5 minutes on cookie sheet or until firm. Remove; cool completely on wire rack.   *Makes about 3 dozen cookies*

Chocolate-Dipped Oat Drops: In medium heavy saucepan over low heat, stir 1½ cups (9 ounces) semisweet chocolate chips until melted and smooth. Dip half of each cookie in melted chocolate. Place on waxed paper to cool.

Tip: Use your microwave oven to eliminate the risks of melting chocolate on top of the stove. To melt 1 (1-ounce) square, microwave on HIGH (100%) 1 to 2 minutes. For 2 squares, 1½ to 2½ minutes is sufficient. For chocolate chips, allow 1½ to 2½ minutes for 1 cup (6 ounces). Remember that the chocolate will not lose its shape in the microwave oven, so stir often to avoid overheating.

Prep Time: 20 minutes
Bake Time: 15 minutes, plus cooling

Super Chocolate Cookies

2 cups all-purpose flour
⅓ cup unsweetened cocoa powder
1 teaspoon baking soda
½ teaspoon salt
1⅓ cups packed light brown sugar
½ cup (1 stick) butter, softened
½ cup shortening
2 eggs
2 teaspoons vanilla
1 cup candy-coated chocolate pieces
1 cup raisins
¾ cup salted peanuts

1. Preheat oven to 350°F. Combine flour, cocoa, baking soda and salt in medium bowl; set aside.

2. Beat brown sugar, butter and shortening in large bowl with electric mixer at medium speed until light and fluffy. Add eggs and vanilla; beat until well blended. Gradually add flour mixture, beating at low speed until blended. Stir in chocolate pieces, raisins and peanuts.

3. Drop dough by ¼ cupfuls 3 inches apart onto ungreased cookie sheets. Flatten slightly with fingertips. Bake 13 to 15 minutes or until almost set. Let cookies cool on cookie sheets 2 minutes; remove to wire racks to cool completely.   *Makes about 20 (4-inch) cookies*

Gift Idea: For small thank-you gifts, party favors or stocking stuffers, place 2 to 4 cookies in cellophane bags or small plastic food storage bags. (Use the kind without a zipper.) Gather the tops and secure the bags with silk flowers or holiday greenery on flexible wire stems.

Super Chocolate Cookies

Choco-Peanut Butter-Brickle Cookies

1 (14-ounce) can **EAGLE BRAND®** Sweetened Condensed Milk
   (NOT evaporated milk)
1 cup chunky peanut butter
2 eggs
1 teaspoon vanilla extract
1½ cups all-purpose flour
1 teaspoon baking soda
½ teaspoon baking powder
½ teaspoon salt
1 cup (6 ounces) semi-sweet chocolate chips
1 cup almond brickle chips or chocolate-covered toffee bits

1. Preheat oven to 350°F. In large bowl, beat EAGLE BRAND®, peanut butter, eggs and vanilla until well blended.

2. In medium bowl, combine flour, baking soda, baking powder and salt; add to peanut butter mixture, beating until blended. Stir in chocolate chips and brickle chips. Drop by heaping tablespoonfuls onto lightly greased baking sheets.

3. Bake 12 minutes or until lightly browned. Cool slightly on baking sheets; remove to wire racks to cool. *Makes 3 dozen cookies*

Prep Time: 15 minutes

Choco-Peanut Butter-Brickle Cookies

Moon Rocks

1 package (18¼ ounces) devil's food or German chocolate cake mix
    with pudding in the mix
3 eggs
½ cup (1 stick) butter, melted
2 cups slightly crushed (2½-inch) pretzel sticks
1½ cups uncooked old-fashioned oats
1 cup swirled chocolate and white chocolate chips or candy-coated
    semisweet chocolate baking pieces

1. Preheat oven to 350°F. Blend cake mix, eggs and butter in large bowl. Stir in crushed pretzels, oats and chips. (Dough will be stiff.)

2. Drop dough by rounded teaspoonfuls about 2 inches apart onto ungreased cookie sheets.

3. Bake 7 to 9 minutes or until set. Let cookies cool on cookie sheets 1 minute; remove to wire racks to cool completely.   *Makes about 5 dozen cookies*

Chocolate-Pecan Angels

1 cup mini semisweet chocolate chips
1 cup chopped pecans, toasted
1 cup sifted powdered sugar
1 egg white

1. Preheat oven to 350°F. Grease cookie sheets. Combine chocolate chips, pecans and powdered sugar in medium bowl. Add egg white; mix well.

2. Drop dough by teaspoonfuls 2 inches apart onto prepared cookie sheets.

3. Bake 11 to 12 minutes or until edges are light golden brown. Let cookies cool on cookie sheets 1 minute; remove to wire racks to cool completely.
Makes about 3 dozen cookies

Moon Rocks

Milk Chocolate Florentine Cookies

⅔ cup butter
2 cups quick oats
1 cup granulated sugar
⅔ cup all-purpose flour
¼ cup light or dark corn syrup
¼ cup milk
1 teaspoon vanilla extract
¼ teaspoon salt
1¾ cups (11.5-ounce package) NESTLÉ® TOLL HOUSE®
   Milk Chocolate Morsels

PREHEAT oven to 375°F. Line baking sheets with foil.

MELT butter in medium saucepan; remove from heat. Stir in oats, sugar, flour, corn syrup, milk, vanilla extract and salt; mix well. Drop by level teaspoon, about 3 inches apart, onto prepared baking sheets. Spread thinly with rubber spatula.

BAKE for 6 to 8 minutes or until golden brown. Cool completely on baking sheets on wire racks. Peel foil from cookies.

MICROWAVE morsels in medium, uncovered, microwave-safe bowl on MEDIUM-HIGH (70%) power for 1 minute. Stir. Morsels may retain some of their original shape. If necessary, microwave at additional 10- to 15-second intervals, stirring just until morsels are melted. Spread thin layer of melted chocolate onto flat side of *half* the cookies. Top with *remaining* cookies.   *Makes about 3½ dozen sandwich cookies*

Milk Chocolate Florentine Cookies

Quick Chocolate Softies

1 package (18¼ ounces) devil's food cake mix
⅓ cup water
¼ cup (½ stick) butter, softened
1 egg
1 cup white chocolate chips
½ cup coarsely chopped walnuts

1. Preheat oven to 350°F. Grease cookie sheets; set aside.

2. Beat cake mix, water, butter and egg in large bowl with electric mixer at low speed until moistened. Increase speed to medium; beat 1 minute. (Dough will be stiff.) Stir in white chocolate chips and nuts; stir until well blended. Drop dough by heaping teaspoonfuls 2 inches apart onto prepared cookie sheets.

3. Bake 10 to 12 minutes or until set. Let cookies cool on cookie sheets 1 minute; remove to wire racks to cool completely.

Makes about 4 dozen cookies

Chocolate Walnut Meringues

3 egg whites
Pinch of salt
¾ cup sugar
½ cup good-quality Dutch-processed cocoa
⅓ cup finely chopped California walnuts

Preheat oven to 350°F. Place egg whites and salt in large mixing bowl. Beat with electric mixer or wire whisk until soft peaks form. Gradually add sugar, beating until stiff peaks form. Sift cocoa over peaks and fold into egg white mixture with walnuts. Spoon mounds about 1 inch in diameter 1 inch apart onto parchment-lined baking sheets. Bake 20 minutes or until dry to the touch. Let cool completely before removing from baking sheets. Store in airtight container.

Makes 4 dozen cookies

Favorite recipe from **Walnut Marketing Board**

Quick Chocolate Softies

Hershey's "Perfectly Chocolate" Chocolate Chip Cookies

1 cup (2 sticks) butter or margarine, softened
¾ cup granulated sugar
¾ cup packed light brown sugar
1 teaspoon vanilla extract
2 eggs
2¼ cups all-purpose flour
⅓ cup HERSHEY'S Cocoa
1 teaspoon baking soda
½ teaspoon salt
2 cups (12-ounce package) HERSHEY'S Semi-Sweet Chocolate Chips
1 cup chopped nuts (optional)

1. Heat oven to 375°F.

2. Beat butter, granulated sugar, brown sugar and vanilla in large bowl until creamy. Add eggs; beat well. Stir together flour, cocoa, baking soda and salt; gradually add to butter mixture, beating until well blended. Stir in chocolate chips and nuts, if desired. Drop by rounded teaspoons onto ungreased cookie sheet.

3. Bake 8 to 10 minutes or until set. Cool slightly; remove from cookie sheet to wire rack. Cool completely. *Makes about 5 dozen cookies*

Hershey's "Perfectly Chocolate" Chocolate Chip Cookies

Chewy Brownie Cookies

1½ cups firmly packed light brown sugar
⅔ CRISCO® Stick or ⅔ cup CRISCO® Shortening
1 tablespoon water
1 teaspoon vanilla
2 eggs
1½ cups PILLSBURY BEST® All-Purpose Flour
⅓ cup unsweetened baking cocoa
½ teaspoon salt
¼ teaspoon baking soda
2 cups semisweet chocolate chips (12-ounce package)

1. Heat oven to 375°F. Place sheets of foil on countertop for cooling cookies.

2. Combine brown sugar, shortening, water and vanilla in large bowl. Beat at medium speed of electric mixer until well blended. Beat eggs into creamed mixture.

3. Combine flour, cocoa, salt and baking soda. Mix into creamed mixture at low speed just until blended. Stir in chocolate chips.

4. Drop rounded measuring tablespoonfuls of dough 2 inches apart onto ungreased baking sheet.

5. Bake one baking sheet at a time at 375°F for 7 to 9 minutes or until cookies are set. *Do not overbake.* Cool 2 minutes on baking sheet. Remove cookies to foil to cool completely.   *Makes about 3 dozen cookies*

Double Chocolate Banana Cookies

3 to 4 extra-ripe medium DOLE® Bananas
2 cups rolled oats
2 cups sugar
1¾ cups all-purpose flour
½ cup unsweetened cocoa powder
1 teaspoon baking soda
½ teaspoon salt
1¼ cups margarine, melted
2 eggs, lightly beaten
2 cups semisweet chocolate chips
1 cup chopped almonds, toasted

• Purée bananas in blender; measure 2 cups for recipe.

• Combine oats, sugar, flour, cocoa, baking soda and salt until well mixed. Stir in bananas, margarine and eggs until blended. Stir in chocolate chips and almonds.

• Refrigerate batter 1 hour or until mixture becomes partially firm (batter runs during baking if too soft).

• Preheat oven to 350°F. Measure ¼ cup batter for each cookie; drop onto greased cookie sheets. Flatten slightly with spatula.

• Bake 15 to 17 minutes until cookies are golden brown. Remove to wire racks to cool. *Makes about 2½ dozen (3-inch) cookies*

Prep Time: 15 minutes
Chill Time: 1 hour
Bake Time: 17 minutes per batch

27

Fudgey Coconut Clusters

5⅓ cups MOUNDS® Sweetened Coconut Flakes
  1 can (14 ounces) sweetened condensed milk (not evaporated milk)
  ⅔ cup HERSHEY'S Cocoa
  ¼ cup (½ stick) butter, melted
  2 teaspoons vanilla extract
  1½ teaspoons almond extract
    HERSHEY'S MINI KISSES® Brand Milk Chocolates or candied
    cherry halves (optional)

1. Heat oven to 350°F. Line cookie sheets with aluminum foil; generously grease foil with vegetable shortening.

2. Combine coconut, sweetened condensed milk, cocoa, melted butter, vanilla and almond extract in large bowl; mix well. Drop by rounded tablespoons onto prepared cookie sheets.

3. Bake 9 to 11 minutes or just until set; press 3 milk chocolates or candied cherry halves in center of each cookie, if desired. Immediately remove cookies to wire rack and cool completely.

Makes about 2½ dozen cookies

Chocolate Chip Macaroons: Omit melted butter and cocoa; stir together other ingredients. Add 1 cup HERSHEY'S MINI CHIPS™ Semi-Sweet Chocolate Chips. Bake 9 to 11 minutes or just until set. Immediately remove to wire racks and cool completely.

Fudgey Coconut Clusters

No-Bake Peanutty Chocolate Drops

½ cup (1 stick) butter or margarine
⅓ cup unsweetened cocoa
2½ cups quick-cooking oats
1 (14-ounce) can EAGLE BRAND® Sweetened Condensed Milk
    (NOT evaporated milk)
1 cup chopped peanuts
½ cup peanut butter

1. Line baking sheets with wax paper. In medium saucepan over medium heat, melt butter; stir in cocoa. Bring mixture to a boil.

2. Remove from heat; stir in remaining ingredients.

3. Drop by teaspoonfuls onto prepared baking sheets; chill 2 hours or until set. Store loosely covered in refrigerator.

Makes about 5 dozen cookies

Prep Time: 10 minutes
Chill Time: 2 hours

Devil's Food Fudge Cookies

1 package DUNCAN HINES® Moist Deluxe® Devil's Food Cake Mix
2 eggs
½ cup vegetable oil
1 cup semisweet chocolate chips
½ cup chopped walnuts

1. Preheat oven to 350°F. Grease baking sheets.

2. Combine cake mix, eggs and oil in large bowl. Beat until well blended. Stir in chocolate chips and walnuts. (Mixture will be stiff.) Shape dough into 36 (1¼-inch) balls. Place 2 inches apart on prepared baking sheets.

3. Bake at 350°F for 10 to 11 minutes. (Cookies will look moist.) *Do not overbake.* Cool 2 minutes on baking sheets. Remove to cooling racks. Cool completely. Store in airtight container. *Makes 3 dozen cookies*

Tip: For a delicious flavor treat, substitute peanut butter chips for the chocolate chips and chopped peanuts for the chopped walnuts.

No-Bake Peanutty Chocolate Drops

Chocolate Pistachio Cookies

2 cups shelled pistachio or macadamia nuts, finely chopped, divided
1¾ cups all-purpose flour
¼ cup unsweetened cocoa powder
¾ teaspoon baking soda
½ teaspoon salt
¾ cup plus 1 tablespoon I CAN'T BELIEVE IT'S NOT BUTTER!®
    Spread, divided
1 cup granulated sugar
¾ cup firmly packed brown sugar
2 eggs
3 squares (1 ounce each) unsweetened chocolate, melted
½ teaspoon vanilla extract
⅛ teaspoon almond extract
1½ squares (1 ounce each) unsweetened chocolate
2 tablespoons confectioners' sugar

Preheat oven to 375°F. Lightly spray baking sheets with I Can't Believe It's Not Butter!® Spray; set aside. Reserve 3 tablespoons pistachios for garnish.

In medium bowl, combine flour, cocoa powder, baking soda and salt; set aside.

In large bowl with electric mixer, beat ¾ cup I Can't Believe It's Not Butter!® Spread, granulated sugar and brown sugar until light and fluffy, about 5 minutes. Beat in eggs, one at a time, beating 30 seconds after each addition. Beat in melted chocolate and extracts. Beat in flour mixture just until blended. Stir in pistachios.

On prepared baking sheets, drop dough by rounded tablespoonfuls 1 inch apart. Bake one sheet at a time 8 minutes or until tops are puffed and dry but still soft when touched. *Do not overbake.* On wire rack, cool 5 minutes; remove from sheets and cool completely.

For icing, in microwave-safe bowl, melt 1½ squares chocolate with remaining 1 tablespoon I Can't Believe It's Not Butter! Spread at HIGH (100%) 1 minute or until chocolate is melted; stir until smooth. Stir in confectioners' sugar. Lightly spread ¼ teaspoon icing on each cookie, then sprinkle with reserved pistachios. Let stand 20 minutes before serving.

Makes about 3½ dozen cookies

Chocolate Pistachio Cookies

Brownies & Bars

White Chocolate Squares

1 (12-ounce) package white chocolate chips, divided
¼ cup (½ stick) butter or margarine
1 (14-ounce) can EAGLE BRAND® Sweetened Condensed Milk
    (NOT evaporated milk)
1 egg
1 teaspoon vanilla extract
2 cups all-purpose flour
½ teaspoon baking powder
1 cup chopped pecans, toasted
    Powdered sugar

1. Preheat oven to 350°F. Grease 13×9-inch baking pan. In large saucepan over low heat, melt 1 cup chips and butter. Stir in EAGLE BRAND®, egg and vanilla. Stir in flour and baking powder until blended. Stir in pecans and remaining chips. Spoon mixture into prepared pan.

2. Bake 20 to 25 minutes. Cool. Sprinkle with powdered sugar; cut into squares. Store covered at room temperature.   *Makes 2 dozen squares*

Prep Time: 15 minutes
Bake Time: 20 to 25 minutes

Clockwise from top left: White Chocolate Squares,
Hershey's Best Brownies (page 36), Chocolatey
Raspberry Crumb Bars (page 38)
and Magic Cookie Bars (page 44)

Hershey's Best Brownies

1 cup (2 sticks) butter or margarine
2 cups sugar
2 teaspoons vanilla extract
4 eggs
¾ cup HERSHEY'S Cocoa or HERSHEY'S SPECIAL DARK® Cocoa
1 cup all-purpose flour
½ teaspoon baking powder
¼ teaspoon salt
1 cup chopped nuts (optional)

1. Heat oven to 350°F. Grease 13×9×2-inch baking pan.

2. Place butter in large microwave-safe bowl. Microwave at HIGH (100%) 2 to 2½ minutes or until melted. Stir in sugar and vanilla. Add eggs, one at a time, beating well with spoon after each addition. Add cocoa; beat until well blended. Add flour, baking powder and salt; beat well. Stir in nuts, if desired. Pour batter into prepared pan.

3. Bake 30 to 35 minutes or until brownies begin to pull away from sides of pan. Cool completely in pan on wire rack. Cut into bars.

Makes about 36 brownies

Crispy Cocoa Bars

¼ cup (½ stick) margarine
¼ cup HERSHEY'S Cocoa
5 cups miniature marshmallows
5 cups crisp rice cereal

1. Spray 13×9×2-inch pan with vegetable cooking spray.

2. Melt margarine in large saucepan over low heat; stir in cocoa and marshmallows. Cook over low heat, stirring constantly, until marshmallows are melted and mixture is smooth and well blended. Continue cooking 1 minute, stirring constantly. Remove from heat.

3. Add cereal; stir until coated. Lightly spray spatula with vegetable cooking spray; press mixture into prepared pan. Cool completely. Cut into bars.

Makes 24 bars

Hershey's Best Brownies

Chocolatey Raspberry Crumb Bars

1 cup (2 sticks) butter or margarine, softened
2 cups all-purpose flour
½ cup packed light brown sugar
¼ teaspoon salt
**2 cups (12-ounce package) NESTLÉ® TOLL HOUSE® Semi-Sweet
   Chocolate Morsels, *divided***
**1 can (14 ounces) NESTLÉ® CARNATION® Sweetened Condensed
   Milk**
½ cup chopped nuts (optional)
⅓ cup seedless raspberry jam

PREHEAT oven to 350°F. Grease 13×9-inch baking pan.

BEAT butter in large mixer bowl until creamy. Beat in flour, sugar and
salt until crumbly. With floured fingers, press *1¾ cups* crumb mixture
onto bottom of prepared baking pan; reserve *remaining* mixture.

BAKE for 10 to 12 minutes or until edges are golden brown.

MICROWAVE *1 cup* morsels and sweetened condensed milk in medium,
uncovered, microwave-safe bowl on HIGH (100%) power for 1 minute.
STIR. Morsels may retain some of their original shape. If necessary,
microwave at additional 10- to 15-second intervals, stirring just until
morsels are melted. Spread over hot crust.

STIR nuts into *reserved* crumb mixture; sprinkle over chocolate layer. Drop
teaspoonfuls of raspberry jam over crumb mixture. Sprinkle with *remaining*
morsels.

BAKE for 25 to 30 minutes or until center is set. Cool in pan on wire rack.
Cut into bars.   *Makes 3 dozen bars*

Chocolatey Raspberry Crumb Bars

Chocolate Chip Cheesecake Bars

Cookie Base
1¾ cups graham cracker crumbs
½ CRISCO® Butter Flavor Stick or ½ cup CRISCO® Butter Flavor Shortening, melted

Filling
1 cup semisweet chocolate chips
2 packages (8 ounces each) cream cheese, softened
1 cup dairy sour cream
2 cups sugar
2 eggs
2 teaspoons vanilla

Drizzle
⅓ cup semisweet chocolate chips
¾ teaspoon CRISCO® Butter Flavor Shortening or ¾ teaspoon CRISCO® Butter Flavor Stick

1. Heat oven to 300°F. Place cooling rack on countertop. For cookie base, combine graham cracker crumbs and ½ cup shortening. Press into bottom of ungreased 13×9×2-inch pan.

2. For filling, sprinkle 1 cup chocolate chips over cookie base. Place cream cheese in large bowl. Beat at medium speed of electric mixer until fluffy. Beat in sour cream. Gradually add sugar. Beat until smooth. Beat in eggs and vanilla. Pour over chocolate chips in pan.

3. Bake at 300°F for 60 minutes or until set. *Do not overbake.* Remove pan to cooling rack and cool 15 minutes.

4. For drizzle, melt ⅓ cup chocolate chips and ¾ teaspoon shortening (see Melting/Drizzling Procedure). Drizzle over cheesecake. Cool. Cut into bars about 2×1¾ inches. Cover. Refrigerate.   *Makes about 2½ dozen bars*

Melting/Drizzling Procedure: For melting or drizzling, choose one of these easy methods. Start with chips and CRISCO Butter Flavor Shortening (if called for), then: place in small microwave-safe measuring cup or bowl. Microwave at 50% (MEDIUM). Stir after 1 minute. Repeat until smooth. Drizzle from tip of spoon. **OR,** place in heavy resealable plastic sandwich bag. Seal. Microwave at 50% (MEDIUM). Check every minute until melted. Knead until smooth. Cut tiny tip off corner of bag. Squeeze out to drizzle. **OR,** place in small saucepan. Melt on rangetop on very low heat. Stir until smooth. Drizzle from tip of spoon.

Peanut Butter Fudge Brownie Bars

1 cup (2 sticks) butter or margarine, melted
1½ cups sugar
2 eggs
1 teaspoon vanilla extract
1¼ cups all-purpose flour
⅔ cup HERSHEY'S Cocoa
¼ cup milk
1¼ cups chopped pecans or walnuts, divided
½ cup (1 stick) butter or margarine
1⅔ cups (10-ounce package) REESE'S® Peanut Butter Chips
1 can (14 ounces) sweetened condensed milk (not evaporated milk)
¼ cup HERSHEY'S Semi-Sweet Chocolate Chips

1. Heat oven to 350°F. Grease 13×9×2-inch baking pan.

2. Beat melted butter, sugar, eggs and vanilla in large bowl with electric mixer on medium speed until well blended. Add flour, cocoa and milk; beat until blended. Stir in 1 cup nuts. Spread in prepared pan.

3. Bake 25 to 30 minutes or just until edges begin to pull away from sides of pan. Cool completely in pan on wire rack.

4. Melt ½ cup butter and peanut butter chips in medium saucepan over low heat, stirring constantly. Add sweetened condensed milk, stirring until smooth; pour over baked layer.

5. Place chocolate chips in small microwave-safe bowl. Microwave at HIGH (100%) 45 seconds or just until chips are melted when stirred. Drizzle bars with melted chocolate; sprinkle with remaining ¼ cup nuts. Refrigerate 1 hour or until firm. Cut into bars. Cover; refrigerate leftover bars. *Makes 36 bars*

Almond Brownies

½ cup (1 stick) butter
2 squares (1 ounce each) unsweetened baking chocolate
2 large eggs
1 cup firmly packed light brown sugar
¼ teaspoon almond extract
½ cup all-purpose flour
1½ cups "M&M's"® Chocolate Mini Baking Bits, divided
½ cup slivered almonds, toasted and divided
    Chocolate Glaze (recipe follows)

Preheat oven to 350°F. Grease and flour 8×8×2-inch baking pan; set aside. In small saucepan melt butter and chocolate over low heat; stir to blend. Remove from heat; let cool. In medium bowl beat eggs and brown sugar until well blended; stir in chocolate mixture and almond extract. Add flour. Stir in 1 cup "M&M's"® Chocolate Mini Baking Bits and ¼ cup almonds. Spread batter evenly in prepared pan. Bake 25 to 28 minutes or until firm in center. Cool completely on wire rack. Prepare Chocolate Glaze. Spread over brownies; decorate with remaining ½ cup "M&M's"® Chocolate Mini Baking Bits and remaining ¼ cup almonds. Cut into bars. Store in tightly covered container.   *Makes 16 brownies*

Chocolate Glaze: In small saucepan over low heat combine 4 teaspoons water and 1 tablespoon butter until it comes to a boil. Stir in 4 teaspoons unsweetened cocoa powder. Gradually stir in ½ cup powdered sugar until smooth. Remove from heat; stir in ¼ teaspoon vanilla extract. Let glaze cool slightly.

Almond Brownies

Magic Cookie Bars

½ cup (1 stick) butter or margarine
1½ cups graham cracker crumbs
1 (14-ounce) can EAGLE BRAND® Sweetened Condensed Milk
    (NOT evaporated milk)
2 cups (12 ounces) semi-sweet chocolate chips
1⅓ cups flaked coconut
1 cup chopped nuts

1. Preheat oven to 350°F (325°F for glass dish). In 13×9-inch baking pan, melt butter in oven.

2. Sprinkle graham cracker crumbs over butter; pour EAGLE BRAND® evenly over crumbs. Layer evenly with remaining ingredients; press down firmly.

3. Bake 25 minutes or until lightly browned. Cool. Cut into bars. Store loosely covered at room temperature.   *Makes 2 to 3 dozen bars*

7-Layer Magic Cookie Bars: Substitute 1 cup (6 ounces) butterscotch-flavored chips for 1 cup semi-sweet chocolate chips. (Peanut butter-flavored chips or white chocolate chips can be substituted for butterscotch-flavored chips.)

Magic Peanut Cookie Bars: Substitute 2 cups (about ¾ pound) chocolate-covered peanuts for semi-sweet chocolate chips and chopped nuts.

Magic Rainbow Cookie Bars: Substitute 2 cups plain candy-coated chocolate pieces for semi-sweet chocolate chips.

Prep Time: 10 minutes
Bake Time: 25 minutes

Magic Cookie Bars

Easy Double Chocolate Chip Brownies

2 cups (12-ounce package) NESTLÉ® TOLL HOUSE® Semi-Sweet
    Chocolate Morsels, *divided*
½ cup (1 stick) butter or margarine, cut into pieces
3 large eggs
1¼ cups all-purpose flour
1 cup granulated sugar
1 teaspoon vanilla extract
¼ teaspoon baking soda
½ cup chopped nuts

PREHEAT oven to 350°F. Grease 13×9-inch baking pan.

MELT *1 cup* morsels and butter in large, *heavy-duty* saucepan over low heat; stir until smooth. Remove from heat. Stir in eggs. Stir in flour, sugar, vanilla extract and baking soda. Stir in *remaining* morsels and nuts. Spread into prepared baking pan.

BAKE for 18 to 22 minutes or until wooden pick inserted in center comes out slightly sticky. Cool completely in pan on wire rack.

Makes 2 dozen brownies

Nutty Chocolate Chunk Bars

3 eggs
1 cup DOMINO® Granulated Sugar
1 cup DOMINO® Brown Sugar, packed
1 cup oat bran
1 cup crunchy peanut butter
¾ cup (1½ sticks) butter, softened
2 teaspoons baking soda
2 teaspoons vanilla
3½ cups quick-cooking oats
1 package (12 ounces) semi-sweet chocolate chunks
1 cup Spanish peanuts

In large bowl, beat eggs, granulated sugar and brown sugar. Add oat bran, peanut butter, butter, baking soda and vanilla. Mix well. Stir in oats, chocolate chunks and peanuts. Spread mixture into greased 15×10×2-inch pan. Bake in 350°F oven 20 to 25 minutes.

Makes 36 bars

Easy Double Chocolate Chip Brownies

Easy Fudgy Mayo Brownies

¾ cup all-purpose flour
½ teaspoon baking powder
¼ teaspoon salt
1 cup (6 ounces) semi-sweet chocolate chips, melted
1 cup sugar
½ cup HELLMANN'S® or BEST FOODS® Real Mayonnaise
2 eggs
1 teaspoon vanilla extract
½ cup chopped walnuts (optional)

1. Preheat oven to 350°F. Grease 8-inch square baking pan with nonstick cooking spray or line with aluminum foil; set aside.

2. In small bowl, combine flour, baking powder and salt; set aside.

3. In large bowl, combine melted chocolate chips, sugar, Hellmann's or Best Foods Real Mayonnaise, eggs and vanilla until smooth. Stir in flour mixture just until blended. Gently stir in walnuts. Spread into prepared pan.

4. Bake 35 minutes or until toothpick inserted 1 inch from edge comes out clean. On wire rack, cool completely. To serve, cut into squares.

Makes 16 servings

Marshmallow Krispie Bars

1 (21-ounce) package DUNCAN HINES® Family-Style Chewy Fudge
   Brownie Mix
1 package (10½ ounces) miniature marshmallows
1½ cups semisweet chocolate chips
1 cup creamy peanut butter
1 tablespoon butter or margarine
1½ cups crisp rice cereal

1. Preheat oven to 350°F. Grease bottom only of 13×9-inch pan.

2. Prepare and bake brownies following package directions for cake-like recipe. Remove from oven. Sprinkle marshmallows on hot brownies. Return to oven. Bake for 3 minutes longer.

3. Place chocolate chips, peanut butter and butter in medium saucepan. Cook over low heat, stirring constantly, until chips are melted. Add rice cereal; mix well. Spread mixture over marshmallow layer. Refrigerate until chilled. Cut into bars. *Makes about 2 dozen bars*

Heavenly Oat Bars

MAZOLA NO STICK® Cooking Spray
½ cup (1 stick) margarine or butter, softened
½ cup firmly packed brown sugar
½ cup KARO® Light or Dark Corn Syrup
1 teaspoon vanilla
3 cups uncooked quick or old-fashioned oats
1 cup (6 ounces) semi-sweet chocolate chips
½ cup creamy peanut butter

1. Preheat oven to 350°F. Spray 9-inch square baking pan with cooking spray.

2. In large bowl with mixer at medium speed, beat margarine, brown sugar, corn syrup and vanilla until blended and smooth. Stir in oats. Spread in prepared pan.

3. Bake 25 minutes or until center is just firm. Cool slightly on wire rack.

4. In small heavy saucepan over low heat, stir chocolate chips until melted and smooth. Remove from heat; stir in peanut butter until smooth. Spread over warm bars. Cool completely in pan on wire rack before cutting.

Makes about 2 dozen bars

Tip: To melt chocolate chips in microwave, place in dry microwavable bowl or glass measuring cup. Microwave on HIGH (100% power) 1 minute; stir. Microwave on HIGH 1 minute longer. Stir until chocolate is smooth.

Prep Time: 15 minutes
Bake Time: 25 minutes, plus cooling

Marvelous Cookie Bars

½ cup (1 stick) butter or margarine, softened
1 cup firmly packed light brown sugar
2 large eggs
1⅓ cups all-purpose flour
1 cup quick-cooking or old-fashioned oats, uncooked
⅓ cup unsweetened cocoa powder
1 teaspoon baking powder
½ teaspoon salt
¼ teaspoon baking soda
½ cup chopped walnuts, divided
1 cup "M&M's"® Semi-Sweet Chocolate Mini Baking Bits, divided
½ cup cherry preserves
¼ cup shredded coconut

Preheat oven to 350°F. Lightly grease 9×9×2-inch baking pan; set aside. In large bowl cream butter and sugar until light and fluffy; beat in eggs. In medium bowl combine flour, oats, cocoa powder, baking powder, salt and baking soda; blend into creamed mixture. Stir in ¼ cup nuts and ¾ cup "M&M's"® Semi-Sweet Chocolate Mini Baking Bits. Reserve 1 cup dough; spread remaining dough into prepared pan. Combine preserves, coconut and remaining ¼ cup nuts; spread evenly over dough to within ½ inch of edge. Drop reserved dough by rounded teaspoonfuls over preserves mixture; sprinkle with remaining ¼ cup "M&M's"® Semi-Sweet Chocolate Mini Baking Bits. Bake 25 to 30 minutes or until slightly firm near edges. Cool completely. Cut into bars. Store in tightly covered container.

Makes 16 bars

Marvelous Cookie Bars

Chunky Caramel Nut Brownies

¾ cup (1½ sticks) butter
4 squares (1 ounce each) unsweetened chocolate
2 cups sugar
4 eggs
1 cup all-purpose flour
1 package (14 ounces) caramels
¼ cup heavy cream
2 cups pecan halves or coarsely chopped pecans, divided
1 package (12 ounces) chocolate chunks or chips

1. Preheat oven to 350°F. Grease 13×9-inch baking pan; set aside.

2. Place butter and chocolate in large microwavable bowl. Microwave on HIGH 1½ to 2 minutes or until chocolate is melted and mixture is smooth when stirred. Stir in sugar until well blended. Beat in eggs, one at a time. Stir in flour until well blended. Spread half of batter in prepared pan. Bake 20 minutes.

3. Meanwhile, combine caramels and cream in medium microwavable bowl. Microwave on HIGH 1½ to 2 minutes or until caramels begin to melt; stir until mixture is smooth. Stir in 1 cup pecan halves.

4. Spread caramel mixture over partially baked brownie base. Sprinkle with half of chocolate chunks. Pour remaining brownie batter over top; sprinkle with remaining 1 cup pecan halves and chocolate chunks. Bake 25 to 30 minutes or until set. Cool in pan on wire rack.

Makes 2 dozen brownies

Chunky Caramel Nut Brownies

Chocolate Nut Bars

1¾ cups graham cracker crumbs
½ cup (1 stick) butter or margarine, melted
2 cups (12 ounces) semi-sweet chocolate chips, divided
1 (14-ounce) can EAGLE BRAND® Sweetened Condensed Milk
    (NOT evaporated milk)
1 teaspoon vanilla extract
1 cup chopped nuts

1. Preheat oven to 375°F. In medium bowl, combine graham cracker crumbs and butter; press firmly on bottom of ungreased 13×9-inch baking pan. Bake 8 minutes. Reduce oven temperature to 350°F.

2. In small saucepan, melt 1 cup chips with EAGLE BRAND® and vanilla. Spread chocolate mixture over prepared crust. Top with remaining 1 cup chips and nuts; press down firmly.

3. Bake 25 to 30 minutes. Cool. Chill, if desired. Cut into bars. Store loosely covered at room temperature.   *Makes 2 to 3 dozen bars*

Prep Time: 10 minutes
Bake Time: 33 to 38 minutes

Chocolate Peanutty Crumble Bars

½ cup (1 stick) butter or margarine
1 cup all-purpose flour
¾ cup quick-cooking oats, uncooked
⅓ cup firmly packed brown sugar
½ teaspoon baking soda
½ teaspoon vanilla extract
4 SNICKERS® Bars (2.07 ounces each), cut into 8 slices each

Preheat oven to 350°F. Grease bottom of 8-inch square baking pan. Melt butter in large saucepan. Remove from heat; stir in flour, oats, brown sugar, baking soda and vanilla. Blend until crumbly. Press ⅔ of mixture into prepared pan. Arrange SNICKERS® Bar slices in pan, about ½ inch from edge of pan. Finely crumble remaining mixture over sliced SNICKERS® Bars. Bake for 25 minutes or until edges are golden brown. Cool in pan on cooling rack. Cut into bars or squares to serve.   *Makes 24 bars*

Chocolate Nut Bars

No-Bake Chocolate Peanut Butter Bars

2 cups peanut butter, *divided*
¾ cup (1½ sticks) butter, softened
2 cups powdered sugar
3 cups graham cracker crumbs
2 cups (12-ounce package) NESTLÉ® TOLL HOUSE® Semi-Sweet Chocolate Mini Morsels, *divided*

GREASE 13×9-inch baking pan.

BEAT *1¼* cups peanut butter and butter in large mixer bowl until creamy. Gradually beat in *1 cup* powdered sugar. With hands or wooden spoon, work in *remaining* powdered sugar, graham cracker crumbs and *½ cup* morsels. Press evenly into prepared pan. Smooth top with spatula.

MELT *remaining* peanut butter and *remaining* morsels in medium, *heavy-duty* saucepan over *lowest possible heat,* stirring constantly, until smooth. Spread over graham cracker crust in pan. Refrigerate for at least 1 hour or until chocolate is firm; cut into bars. Store in refrigerator.

Makes 5 dozen bars

Pop Corn S'Mores

2 quarts popped JOLLY TIME® Pop Corn
15 graham cracker squares
4 cups miniature marshmallows, divided
1 cup semi-sweet chocolate pieces
2 tablespoons butter or margarine

Preheat oven to 350°F. Put popped pop corn in large bowl. Arrange graham cracker squares in bottom of 13×9-inch baking pan; trim slightly if necessary to fit pan. Sprinkle with 2 cups marshmallows and chocolate pieces. Place butter in 2-quart glass measuring pitcher. Microwave at HIGH (100% power) until butter is melted, about 45 seconds. Stir in remaining 2 cups marshmallows until well coated. Microwave at HIGH (100% power) until marshmallows look puffy, about 1 minute; stir to melt completely. Pour marshmallow mixture over popped pop corn and mix well. Spread coated pop corn evenly over chocolate pieces in pan. Bake until marshmallows are puffy and appear to be melted, about 6 minutes. Invert pan onto cutting board and cut into squares between graham crackers.   *Makes 15 bars*

No-Bake Chocolate Peanut Butter Bars

Buried Cherry Bars

1 jar (10 ounces) maraschino cherries
1 package (18¼ ounces) devil's food cake mix *without* pudding in
   the mix
1 cup (2 sticks) butter, melted
1 egg
½ teaspoon almond extract
1½ cups semisweet chocolate chips
¾ cup sweetened condensed milk
½ cup chopped pecans

1. Preheat oven to 350°F. Lightly grease 13×9-inch baking pan. Drain maraschino cherries, reserving 2 tablespoons juice. Cut cherries into quarters.

2. Combine cake mix, butter, egg and almond extract in large bowl; mix well. (Batter will be very thick.) Spread batter in prepared pan. Lightly press cherries into batter.

3. Combine chocolate chips and sweetened condensed milk in small saucepan. Cook over low heat, stirring constantly, until chocolate melts. Stir in reserved cherry juice. Spread chocolate mixture over cherries in pan; sprinkle with pecans.

4. Bake 35 minutes or until almost set in center. Cool completely in pan on wire rack.   *Makes 2 dozen bars*

Buried Cherry Bars

Chocolate Almond Macaroon Bars

2 cups chocolate wafer cookie crumbs
6 tablespoons butter or margarine, melted
6 tablespoons powdered sugar
1 can (14 ounces) sweetened condensed milk
3¾ cups MOUNDS® Sweetened Coconut Flakes
1 cup sliced almonds, toasted* (optional)
1 cup HERSHEY₃S Semi-Sweet Chocolate Chips
¼ cup whipping cream
½ cup HERSHEY₃S Premier White Chips

*To toast almonds, heat oven to 350°F. Spread almonds evenly on shallow baking sheet. Bake 5 to 8 minutes or until lightly browned.

1. Heat oven to 350°F. Grease 13×9×2-inch baking pan.

2. Combine crumbs, melted butter and sugar in large bowl. Firmly press crumb mixture on bottom of prepared pan. Stir together sweetened condensed milk, coconut and almonds in large bowl, mixing well. Carefully drop mixture by spoonfuls over crust; spread evenly.

3. Bake 20 to 25 minutes or until coconut edges just begin to brown. Cool.

4. Place chocolate chips and whipping cream in medium microwave-safe bowl. Microwave at HIGH (100%) 1 minute; stir. If necessary, microwave at HIGH an additional 10 seconds at a time, stirring after each heating, until chips are melted and mixture is smooth when stirred. Cool until slightly thickened; spread over cooled bars. Sprinkle top with white chips. Cover; refrigerate several hours or until thoroughly chilled. Cut into bars. Refrigerate leftovers.   *Makes about 36 bars*

Chocolate Almond Macaroon Bars

Sinfully Rich Cakes

Chocolate Almond Torte

4 eggs, separated
½ cup (1 stick) butter or margarine, softened
1 cup sugar
1 teaspoon almond extract
1 teaspoon vanilla extract
1 cup finely chopped toasted almonds
¾ cup all-purpose flour
½ cup unsweetened cocoa
½ teaspoon baking powder
½ teaspoon baking soda
⅔ cup milk
  Chocolate Almond Frosting (page 64)

1. Line 2 (8- or 9-inch) round cake pans with waxed paper. Preheat oven to 350°F. In small bowl, beat egg whites until soft peaks form; set aside.

2. In large bowl, beat butter and sugar until fluffy. Add egg yolks and extracts; mix well.

continued on page 64

Clockwise from top left: Chocolate Almond Torte, Chocolate Intensity (page 70), Hot Fudge Sundae Cake (page 66) and Chocolate Lava Cake (page 68)

Chocolate Almond Torte, continued

3. In medium bowl, combine almonds, flour, cocoa, baking powder and baking soda; add alternately with milk to butter mixture, beating well after each addition.

4. Fold in beaten egg whites. Pour into prepared pans. Bake 18 to 20 minutes or until wooden picks inserted near centers come out clean. Cool 10 minutes; remove from pans. Cool completely.

5. Prepare Chocolate Almond Frosting. Split each cake layer; fill and frost with frosting. Garnish as desired. Store covered in refrigerator.

Makes one 4-layer cake

Prep Time: 30 minutes
Bake Time: 18 to 20 minutes

Chocolate Almond Frosting

2 (1-ounce) squares semi-sweet chocolate, chopped
1 (14-ounce) can EAGLE BRAND® Sweetened Condensed Milk (NOT evaporated milk)
1 teaspoon almond extract

1. In heavy saucepan over medium heat, melt chocolate with EAGLE BRAND®. Cook and stir until mixture thickens, about 10 minutes.

2. Remove from heat; cool 10 minutes. Stir in almond extract; cool.

Makes about 1½ cups

Prep Time: 20 minutes

Chocolate Raspberry Cake

4 (1-ounce) squares unsweetened chocolate
¼ cup water
½ cup butter or margarine, cut into small pieces
½ cup sugar
3 eggs, separated
⅓ cup unsifted all-purpose flour
½ cup SMUCKER'S® Red Raspberry Preserves
Chocolate shavings (see Note)
Fresh raspberries

Grease and flour two 8-inch round cake pans; set aside. In medium saucepan, melt chocolate and water over low heat, stirring constantly. Add butter; stir until completely melted. Remove from heat and blend in sugar; cool.

Add egg yolks, one at a time, beating well after each addition. Add flour to chocolate mixture; blend well. Beat egg whites until stiff but not dry; fold into chocolate mixture. Pour into prepared cake pans.

Bake in preheated 325°F oven about 25 minutes or until toothpick inserted into center of cake layer comes out clean. Cool 10 minutes on wire rack; remove layers from pans. Cool completely.

Heat preserves in saucepan until melted. Spread half of preserves on first layer. Top with second layer; spread with remaining preserves. Garnish with chocolate shavings and raspberries. *Makes 12 to 15 servings*

Note: For chocolate shavings, melt 1 to 2 ounces semisweet chocolate. Spread melted chocolate in thin layer on baking sheet; refrigerate until set. Scrape with metal spatula held at 45° angle to produce shavings and curls. Chill or freeze shavings until ready to use.

Hot Fudge Sundae Cake

1 package DUNCAN HINES® Moist Deluxe® Dark Chocolate Fudge Cake Mix
½ gallon brick vanilla ice cream

Fudge Sauce
1 can (12 ounces) evaporated milk
1¼ cups sugar
4 squares (1 ounce each) unsweetened chocolate
¼ cup butter or margarine
1½ teaspoons vanilla extract
¼ teaspoon salt
Whipped cream and maraschino cherries for garnish

1. Preheat oven to 350°F. Grease and flour 13×9×2-inch pan. Prepare, bake and cool cake following package directions.

2. Remove cake from pan. Split cake in half horizontally. Place bottom layer back in pan. Cut ice cream into even slices and place evenly over bottom cake layer (use all the ice cream). Place remaining cake layer over ice cream. Cover and freeze.

3. For fudge sauce, combine evaporated milk and sugar in medium saucepan. Cook, stirring constantly, over medium heat until mixture comes to a rolling boil. Boil and stir for 1 minute. Add unsweetened chocolate and stir until melted. Beat over medium heat until smooth. Remove from heat. Stir in butter, vanilla extract and salt.

4. Cut cake into squares. For each serving, place cake square on plate; spoon hot fudge sauce on top. Garnish with whipped cream and maraschino cherry.

Makes 12 to 16 servings

Tip: Fudge sauce may be prepared ahead and refrigerated in tightly sealed jar. Reheat when ready to serve.

Hot Fudge Sundae Cake

Chocolate Lava Cakes

6 tablespoons I CAN'T BELIEVE IT'S NOT BUTTER!® Spread
3 squares (1 ounce each) bittersweet or semi-sweet chocolate, cut
    into pieces
½ cup granulated sugar
6 tablespoons all-purpose flour
    Pinch salt
2 eggs
2 egg yolks
¼ teaspoon vanilla extract
    Confectioners' sugar

Line bottom of four (4-ounce) ramekins* or custard cups with waxed paper, then grease; set aside.

In medium microwave-safe bowl, microwave I Can't Believe It's Not Butter!® Spread and chocolate at HIGH (100%) 45 seconds or until chocolate is melted; stir until smooth. With wire whisk, beat in granulated sugar, flour and salt until blended. Beat in eggs, egg yolks and vanilla. Evenly spoon into prepared ramekins. Refrigerate 1 hour or until ready to bake.

Preheat oven to 425°F. Arrange ramekins on baking sheet. Bake 13 minutes or until edges are firm but centers are still slightly soft. (*Do not overbake*). On wire rack, cool 5 minutes. To serve, carefully run sharp knife around cake edges. Unmold onto serving plates, then remove waxed paper. Sprinkle with confectioners' sugar and serve immediately.   *Makes 4 servings*

*To bake in 12-cup muffin pan, line bottoms of 8 muffin cups with waxed paper, then grease. Evenly spoon in batter. Refrigerate as above. Bake at 425°F for 9 minutes or until edges are firm but centers are still slightly soft. Do not overbake. On wire rack, cool 5 minutes. To serve, carefully run sharp knife around cake edges and gently lift out of pan. (Do not turn pan upside-down to unmold.) Arrange cakes, bottom sides up, on serving plates, 2 cakes per serving. Remove waxed paper and sprinkle as above.

Chocolate Lava Cake

Chocolate Intensity

Cake
> **4 bars (8-ounce box) NESTLÉ® TOLL HOUSE® Unsweetened Chocolate Baking Bars, broken into pieces**
> **1½ cups granulated sugar**
> **½ cup (1 stick) butter, softened**
> **3 large eggs**
> **2 teaspoons vanilla extract**
> **⅔ cup all-purpose flour**
> **Powdered sugar (optional)**

Coffee Crème Anglaise Sauce
> **⅓ cup granulated sugar**
> **1 tablespoon TASTER'S CHOICE® 100% Pure Instant Coffee**
> **1½ cups milk**
> **4 large egg yolks, lightly beaten**
> **1 teaspoon vanilla extract**

PREHEAT oven to 350°F. Grease 9-inch springform pan.

For Cake
MICROWAVE baking bars in medium, uncovered, microwave-safe bowl on HIGH (100%) power for 1 minute. STIR. Bars may retain some of their original shape. If necessary, microwave at additional 10- to 15-second intervals, stirring just until smooth. Cool to lukewarm.

BEAT granulated sugar, butter, eggs and vanilla extract in small mixer bowl for about 4 minutes or until thick and pale yellow. Beat in melted chocolate. Gradually beat in flour. Spread into prepared springform pan.

BAKE for 25 to 28 minutes or until wooden pick inserted in center comes out moist. Cool in pan on wire rack for 15 minutes. Loosen and remove side of pan; cool completely. Sprinkle with powdered sugar; serve with Coffee Crème Anglaise Sauce.

For Coffee Crème Anglaise Sauce
COMBINE granulated sugar and Taster's Choice in medium saucepan; stir in milk. Cook over medium heat, stirring constantly, until mixture comes just to a very gentle boil. Remove from heat. Gradually whisk *half* of hot milk mixture into egg yolks; return mixture to saucepan. Cook, stirring constantly, for 3 to 4 minutes or until mixture is slightly thickened. Strain into small bowl; stir in vanilla extract. Cover; refrigerate.

Makes 10 to 12 servings

Fudgy Banana Oat Cake

Topping
 1 cup QUAKER® Oats (quick or old fashioned, uncooked)
 ½ cup firmly packed brown sugar
 ¼ cup (½ stick) margarine or butter, chilled

Filling
 1 cup (6 ounces) semisweet chocolate pieces
 ⅔ cup sweetened condensed milk (not evaporated milk)
 1 tablespoon margarine or butter

Cake
 1 package (18.25 ounces) devil's food cake mix
 1¼ cups mashed ripe bananas (about 3 large)
 ⅓ cup vegetable oil
 3 eggs
 Banana slices (optional)
 Sweetened whipped cream (optional)

Heat oven to 350°F. Lightly grease bottom only of 13×9-inch baking pan. For topping, combine oats and brown sugar. Cut in margarine until mixture is crumbly; set aside.

For filling, in small saucepan, heat chocolate pieces, sweetened condensed milk and margarine over low heat until chocolate is melted, stirring occasionally. Remove from heat; set aside.

For cake, in large mixing bowl, combine cake mix, bananas, oil and eggs. Blend at low speed of electric mixer until dry ingredients are moistened. Beat at medium speed 2 minutes. Spread batter evenly into prepared pan. Drop chocolate filling by teaspoonfuls evenly over batter. Sprinkle with reserved oat topping. Bake 40 to 45 minutes or until cake pulls away from sides of pan and topping is golden brown. Cool cake in pan on wire rack. Cut into squares. Garnish with banana slices and sweetened whipped cream, if desired.   *Makes 15 servings*

Hershey's Red Velvet Cake

½ cup (1 stick) butter or margarine, softened
1½ cups sugar
 2 eggs
 1 teaspoon vanilla extract
 1 cup buttermilk or sour milk*
 2 tablespoons (1-ounce bottle) red food color
 2 cups all-purpose flour
 ⅓ cup HERSHEY'S Cocoa
 1 teaspoon salt
1½ teaspoons baking soda
 1 tablespoon white vinegar
 1 can (16 ounces) ready-to-spread vanilla frosting
   HERSHEY'S MINI CHIPS™ Semi-Sweet Chocolate Chips or
   HERSHEY'S Milk Chocolate Chips (optional)

To sour milk: Use 1 tablespoon white vinegar plus milk to equal 1 cup.

1. Heat oven to 350°F. Grease and flour 13×9×2-inch baking pan.**

2. Beat butter and sugar in large bowl; add eggs and vanilla, beating well. Stir together buttermilk and food color. Stir together flour, cocoa and salt; add alternately to butter mixture with buttermilk mixture, mixing well. Stir in baking soda and vinegar. Pour into prepared pan.

3. Bake 30 to 35 minutes or until wooden pick inserted in center comes out clean. Cool completely in pan on wire rack. Frost; garnish with chocolate chips, if desired.   *Makes about 15 servings*

***This recipe can be made in 2 (9-inch) cake pans. Bake at 350°F for 30 to 35 minutes.*

Hershey's Red Velvet Cake

Triple Chip Cheesecake

Crust
1¾ cups chocolate graham cracker crumbs
⅓ cup butter or margarine, melted

Filling
3 packages (8 ounces *each*) cream cheese, softened
¾ cup granulated sugar
½ cup sour cream
3 tablespoons all-purpose flour
1½ teaspoons vanilla extract
3 eggs
1 cup (6 ounces) NESTLÉ® TOLL HOUSE® Butterscotch Flavored
   Morsels
1 cup (6 ounces) NESTLÉ® TOLL HOUSE® Semi-Sweet Chocolate
   Morsels
1 cup (6 ounces) NESTLÉ® TOLL HOUSE® Premier White Morsels

Topping
1 tablespoon *each* NESTLÉ® TOLL HOUSE® Butterscotch Flavored
   Morsels, Semi-Sweet Chocolate Morsels and Premier White
   Morsels

PREHEAT oven to 300°F. Grease 9-inch springform pan.

For Crust
COMBINE crumbs and butter in small bowl. Press onto bottom and 1 inch
up side of prepared pan.

For Filling
BEAT cream cheese and granulated sugar in large mixer bowl until smooth.
Add sour cream, flour and vanilla extract; mix well. Add eggs; beat on low
speed until combined.

MELT butterscotch morsels according to package directions. Stir until
smooth. Add *1½ cups* batter to melted morsels. Pour into crust. Repeat
procedure with semi-sweet morsels. Carefully spoon over butterscotch layer.
Melt Premier White morsels according to package directions and blend into
remaining batter in mixer bowl. Carefully pour over semi-sweet layer.

BAKE for 1 hour and 10 to 15 minutes or until center is almost set. Cool in
pan on wire rack for 10 minutes. Run knife around edge of cheesecake. Let
stand for 1 hour.

continued on page 76

Triple Chip Cheesecake

Triple Chip Cheesecake, continued

For Topping
PLACE each flavor of morsels separately into three small, *heavy-duty* resealable plastic food storage bags. Microwave on HIGH (100%) power for 20 seconds; knead bags to mix. Microwave at additional 10-second intervals, kneading until smooth. Cut small hole in corner of each bag; squeeze to drizzle over cheesecake. Refrigerate for at least 3 hours or overnight. Remove side of pan.   *Makes 12 to 16 servings*

Chocolate Sheet Cake

1¼ cups (2½ sticks) butter or margarine, divided
1 cup water
½ cup unsweetened cocoa, divided
2 cups all-purpose flour
1½ cups firmly packed light brown sugar
1 teaspoon baking soda
1 teaspoon ground cinnamon
½ teaspoon salt
1 (14-ounce) can EAGLE BRAND® Sweetened Condensed Milk (NOT evaporated milk), divided
2 eggs
1 teaspoon vanilla extract
1 cup powdered sugar
1 cup coarsely chopped nuts

1. Preheat oven to 350°F. In small saucepan over medium heat, melt 1 cup butter; stir in water and ¼ cup cocoa. Bring to a boil; remove from heat. In large bowl, combine flour, brown sugar, baking soda, cinnamon and salt. Add cocoa mixture; beat well. Stir in ⅓ cup EAGLE BRAND®, eggs and vanilla. Pour into greased 15×10×1-inch baking pan. Bake 15 minutes or until cake springs back when lightly touched.

2. In small saucepan, over medium heat, melt remaining ¼ cup butter; add remaining ¼ cup cocoa and remaining EAGLE BRAND®. Stir in powdered sugar and nuts. Spread over warm cake.   *Makes one (15×10-inch) cake*

Super-Moist Chocolate Mayo Cake

1 box (18 ounces) chocolate cake mix
1 cup HELLMANN'S® or BEST FOODS® Real Mayonnaise
1 cup water
3 eggs
1 teaspoon ground cinnamon (optional)

1. Preheat oven to 350°F. Grease and lightly flour two 9-inch round cake pans; set aside.

2. In large bowl, with electric mixer at low speed, beat cake mix, Hellmann's or Best Foods Real Mayonnaise, water, eggs and cinnamon 30 seconds. Beat on medium speed 2 minutes, scraping sides occasionally. Pour into prepared pans.

3. Bake 30 minutes or until toothpick inserted in center comes out clean. On wire rack, cool 10 minutes; remove from pans and cool completely. Sprinkle, if desired, with confectioners sugar or fill and frost.

Makes 12 servings

Pecan Coconut-Topped Cake: Combine 1 cup flaked coconut, ⅔ cup firmly packed brown sugar and ½ cup chopped pecans, then sprinkle over cake batter in 13×9-inch baking pan before baking.

Decadent Chocolate Lava Cake: Combine 2 packages (3.4 ounces each) instant pudding, 2 cups water, 2 cups milk and ⅓ cup sugar until blended, then pour over cake batter in 13×9-inch baking pan. Bake 1 hour or until toothpick inserted along edge comes out clean. Serve warm.

Yellow Mayonnaise Cake: Substitute 1 box (18 ounces) yellow cake mix for chocolate cake mix.

Prep Time: 5 minutes
Cook Time: 30 minutes

Mini Chocolate Cheesecakes

8 squares (1 ounce each) semisweet baking chocolate
3 packages (8 ounces each) cream cheese, softened
½ cup sugar
3 eggs
1 teaspoon vanilla

1. Preheat oven to 325°F. Lightly grease 12 standard (2¾-inch) muffin pan cups; set aside.

2. Place chocolate in 1-cup microwavable bowl. Microwave on HIGH 1 to 1½ minutes or until chocolate is melted, stirring after 1 minute. Let cool slightly.

3. Beat cream cheese and sugar in large bowl with electric mixer at medium speed about 2 minutes or until light and fluffy. Add eggs and vanilla; beat about 2 minutes or until well blended. Beat melted chocolate into cream cheese mixture until well blended.

4. Divide mixture evenly among prepared muffin cups. Place muffin pan in larger baking pan; place on oven rack. Pour warm water into larger pan to depth of ½ to 1 inch. Bake cheesecakes 30 minutes or until edges are dry and centers are almost set. Remove muffin pan from water. Cool cheesecakes completely in muffin pan on wire rack.

Makes 12 cheesecakes

Mini Swirl Cheesecakes: Before adding chocolate to batter in mixer bowl, place about 2 heaping tablespoons of batter into each muffin cup. Add chocolate to remaining batter in mixer bowl and beat to combine. Spoon chocolate batter on top of vanilla batter in muffin cups. Swirl with knife before baking.

Mini Swirl Cheesecakes

Chocolate Squares with Nutty Caramel Sauce

1 cup sugar
¾ cup all-purpose flour
½ cup HERSHEY'S SPECIAL DARK® Cocoa or HERSHEY'S
   Cocoa
½ teaspoon baking powder
½ teaspoon salt
¾ cup vegetable oil
3 eggs
¼ cup milk
½ teaspoon vanilla extract
1 bag (14 ounces) caramel candies
½ cup water
1 cup pecan pieces
   Sweetened whipped cream (optional)

1. Heat oven to 350°F. Grease bottom only of 8-inch square baking pan.

2. Stir together sugar, flour, cocoa, baking powder and salt in medium bowl. Add oil, eggs, milk and vanilla; beat until smooth. Pour batter into prepared pan.

3. Bake 35 to 40 minutes or until wooden pick inserted in center comes out clean. Cool completely in pan on wire rack.

4. Remove wrappers from caramels. Combine caramels and water in small saucepan. Cook over low heat, stirring occasionally, until smooth and well blended. Stir in pecans; cool until thickened slightly. Cut cake into squares; serve with warm caramel nut sauce and sweetened whipped cream, if desired. *Makes 9 servings*

Chocolate Square with Nutty Caramel Sauce

Glazed Chocolate Pound Cake

Cake

1¾ CRISCO® Butter Flavor Sticks or 1¾ cups CRISCO® Butter Flavor
  Shortening plus additional for greasing
  3 cups granulated sugar
  5 eggs
  1 teaspoon vanilla
3¼ cups PILLSBURY BEST® All-Purpose Flour
  ½ cup unsweetened cocoa powder
  1 teaspoon baking powder
  ½ teaspoon salt
1⅓ cups milk
  1 cup miniature semisweet chocolate chips

Glaze

  1 cup miniature semisweet chocolate chips
  ¼ CRISCO® Butter Flavor Stick or ¼ cup CRISCO® Butter Flavor
    Shortening
  1 tablespoon light corn syrup

1. For cake, heat oven to 325°F. Grease and flour 10-inch tube pan.

2. Combine 1¾ cups shortening, sugar, eggs and vanilla in large bowl. Beat at low speed of electric mixer until blended, scraping bowl frequently. Beat at high speed 6 minutes, scraping bowl occasionally. Combine flour, cocoa, baking powder and salt in medium bowl. Mix in dry ingredients alternately with milk, beating after each addition until batter is smooth. Stir in 1 cup chocolate chips. Spoon into prepared pan.

3. Bake at 325°F for 75 to 85 minutes or until toothpick inserted near center comes out clean. Cool on cooling rack 20 minutes. Invert onto serving plate. Cool completely.

4. For glaze, combine 1 cup chocolate chips, ¼ cup shortening and corn syrup in top part of double boiler over hot, not boiling, water. Stir until just melted and smooth. Cool slightly. (Or place mixture in microwave-safe bowl. Microwave at 50% (MEDIUM) for 1 minute and 15 seconds. Stir. Repeat at 15-second intervals, if necessary, until just melted and smooth. Cool slightly.) Spoon glaze over cake. Let stand until glaze is firm.

Makes 1 (10-inch) tube cake

Prep Time: about 30 minutes
Bake Time: 75 to 85 minutes

Glazed Chocolate Pound Cake

Dandy Cake

1 cup water
1 cup (2 sticks) butter or margarine
⅓ cup HERSHEY'S Cocoa
2 cups all-purpose flour
2 cups sugar
1 teaspoon baking soda
½ teaspoon salt
3 eggs
¾ cup dairy sour cream
¾ cup REESE'S® Creamy Peanut Butter
   Chocolate Topping (recipe follows)

1. Heat oven to 350°F. Grease and flour 15½×10½×1-inch jelly-roll pan.

2. Combine water, butter and cocoa in small saucepan. Cook over medium heat, stirring occasionally, until mixture boils; boil and stir 1 minute. Remove from heat; set aside.

3. Stir together flour, sugar, baking soda and salt in large bowl. Add eggs and sour cream; beat until well blended. Add cocoa mixture; beat just until blended (batter will be thin). Pour into prepared pan.

4. Bake 25 to 30 minutes or until wooden pick inserted in center comes out clean. Do not remove cake from pan. Spread peanut butter over warm cake. Cool completely in pan on wire rack. Prepare Chocolate Topping; carefully spread over top, covering peanut butter. Allow topping to set; cut into squares.   *Makes 20 to 24 servings*

Chocolate Topping: Place 2 cups (12-ounce package) HERSHEY'S Semi-Sweet Chocolate Chips and 2 tablespoons shortening (do not use butter, margarine, spread or oil) in small microwave-safe bowl. Microwave at HIGH (100%) 1½ minutes; stir. If necessary, microwave at HIGH an additional 15 seconds at a time, stirring after each heating, just until chips are melted when stirred.

Dandy Cake

Decadent Desserts

Chocolate Peanut Butter Cups

1 package DUNCAN HINES® Moist Deluxe® Swiss Chocolate Cake Mix
1 container DUNCAN HINES® Creamy Home-Style Classic Vanilla Frosting
½ cup creamy peanut butter
15 miniature peanut butter cup candies, wrappers removed, cut in half vertically

1. Preheat oven to 350°F. Place paper liners in 30 (2½-inch) muffin cups.

2. Prepare, bake and cool cupcakes following package directions for basic recipe.

3. Combine Vanilla frosting and peanut butter in medium bowl. Stir until smooth. Frost one cupcake. Decorate with peanut butter cup candy, cut side down. Repeat with remaining cupcakes, frosting and candies.

Makes 30 servings

Tip: You can substitute DUNCAN HINES® Moist Deluxe® Devil's Food, Dark Chocolate Fudge or Butter Recipe Fudge Cake Mix flavors for Swiss Chocolate Cake Mix.

__Clockwise from top left:__ Chocolate Peanut Butter Cups, Chocolate Petits Fours (page 96), Chocolate Mudslide Frozen Pie (page 88) and Chocolate Mint Truffles (page 92)

Chocolate Mudslide Frozen Pie

1 *prepared* 9-inch (6 ounces) chocolate crumb crust
1 cup (6 ounces) NESTLÉ® TOLL HOUSE® Semi-Sweet
   Chocolate Morsels
1 teaspoon TASTER'S CHOICE® 100% Pure Instant Coffee
1 teaspoon hot water
¾ cup sour cream
½ cup granulated sugar
1 teaspoon vanilla extract
1½ cups heavy whipping cream
1 cup powdered sugar
¼ cup NESTLÉ® TOLL HOUSE® Baking Cocoa
2 tablespoons NESTLÉ® TOLL HOUSE® Semi-Sweet Chocolate
   Mini Morsels

MELT *1 cup* morsels in small, *heavy-duty* saucepan over *lowest possible* heat. When morsels begin to melt, remove from heat; stir. Return to heat for a few seconds at a time, stirring until smooth. Remove from heat; cool for 10 minutes.

COMBINE Taster's Choice and water in medium bowl. Add sour cream, granulated sugar and vanilla extract; stir until sugar is dissolved. Stir in melted chocolate until smooth. Spread into crust; refrigerate.

BEAT cream, powdered sugar and cocoa in small mixer bowl until stiff peaks form. Spread or pipe over chocolate layer. Sprinkle with mini morsels. Freeze for at least 6 hours or until firm. *Makes 8 servings*

Chocolate Mudslide Frozen Pie

Cracker Toffee

72 butter-flavored crackers
1 cup (2 sticks) unsalted butter
1 cup packed brown sugar
¼ teaspoon salt
2½ cups semisweet chocolate chips
2 cups chopped pecans

1. Preheat oven to 375°F. Line 17×12-inch jelly-roll pan with heavy-duty foil. Spray generously with nonstick cooking spray. Arrange crackers in pan and set aside.

2. Combine butter, brown sugar and salt in heavy medium saucepan. Heat over medium heat until butter melts, stirring frequently. Increase heat to high; boil 3 minutes without stirring. Pour mixture evenly over crackers; spread to cover.

3. Bake 5 minutes. Immediately sprinkle chocolate chips evenly over crackers; spread to cover. Sprinkle pecans over chocolate, pressing down. Cool to room temperature. Refrigerate 2 hours. Break into chunks to serve.   *Makes 24 servings*

Variation: Substitute peanut butter chips for chocolate chips and coarsely chopped, lightly salted peanuts for chopped pecans.

Easy Homemade Chocolate Ice Cream

1 (14-ounce) can EAGLE BRAND® Sweetened Condensed Milk
(NOT evaporated milk)
⅔ cup chocolate-flavored syrup
2 cups (1 pint) whipping cream, whipped (do not use non-dairy whipped topping)

1. In large bowl, combine EAGLE BRAND® and chocolate syrup; mix well. Fold in whipped cream. Pour into 9×5-inch loaf pan or other 2-quart container; cover.

2. Freeze 6 hours or until firm. Store leftovers in freezer.

Makes about 1½ quarts ice cream

Cracker Toffee

Chocolate Mint Truffles

1¾ cups (11.5-ounce package) NESTLÉ® TOLL HOUSE® Milk
   Chocolate Morsels
1 cup (6 ounces) NESTLÉ® TOLL HOUSE® Semi-Sweet Chocolate
   Morsels
¾ cup heavy whipping cream
1 tablespoon peppermint extract
1½ cups finely chopped walnuts, toasted, or NESTLÉ® TOLL HOUSE®
   Baking Cocoa

LINE baking sheet with wax paper.

PLACE milk chocolate and semi-sweet morsels in large mixer bowl. Heat cream to a gentle boil in small saucepan; pour over morsels. Let stand for 1 minute; stir until smooth. Stir in peppermint extract. Cover with plastic wrap; refrigerate for 35 to 45 minutes or until slightly thickened. Stir just until color lightens slightly. (*Do not* overmix or truffles will be grainy.)

DROP by rounded teaspoon onto prepared baking sheet; refrigerate for 10 to 15 minutes. Shape into balls; roll in walnuts or cocoa. Store in airtight container in refrigerator.   *Makes about 48 truffles*

Variation: After rolling chocolate mixture into balls, freeze for 30 to 40 minutes. Microwave 1¾ cups (11.5-ounce package) NESTLÉ® TOLL HOUSE® Milk Chocolate Morsels and 3 tablespoons vegetable shortening in medium, uncovered, microwave-safe bowl on MEDIUM-HIGH (70%) power for 1 minute. STIR. Morsels may retain some of their original shape. If necessary, microwave at additional 10- to 15-second intervals, stirring just until morsels are melted. Dip truffles into chocolate mixture; shake off excess. Place on foil-lined baking sheets. Refrigerate for 15 to 20 minutes or until set. Store in airtight container in refrigerator.

Chocolate Mint Truffles

Mini Brownie Cups

¼ cup (½ stick) 56 to 60% corn oil spread
2 egg whites
1 egg
¾ cup sugar
⅔ cup all-purpose flour
⅓ cup HERSHEY'S Cocoa
½ teaspoon baking powder
¼ teaspoon salt
  Mocha Glaze (recipe follows)

1. Heat oven to 350°F. Line small muffin cups (1¾ inches in diameter) with paper baking cups or spray with vegetable cooking spray.

2. Melt corn oil spread in small saucepan over low heat; cool slightly. Beat egg whites and egg in small bowl with electric mixer on medium speed until foamy; gradually add sugar, beating until slightly thickened and light in color. Stir together flour, cocoa, baking powder and salt; gradually add to egg mixture, beating until blended. Gradually add corn oil spread, beating just until blended. Fill muffin cups ⅔ full with batter.

3. Bake 15 to 18 minutes or until wooden pick inserted in center comes out clean. Remove from pan to wire rack. Cool completely. Prepare Mocha Glaze; drizzle over tops of brownie cups. Let stand until glaze is set.

Makes 24 servings

Mocha Glaze

¼ cup powdered sugar
¾ teaspoon HERSHEY'S Cocoa
¼ teaspoon powdered instant coffee
2 teaspoons hot water
¼ teaspoon vanilla extract

1. Stir together powdered sugar and cocoa in small bowl. Dissolve coffee in water; gradually add to sugar mixture, stirring until well blended. Stir in vanilla.

Mini Brownie Cups

Chocolate Petits Fours

1 package DUNCAN HINES® Moist Deluxe® Dark Chocolate Fudge
  Cake Mix
1 package (7 ounces) pure almond paste
½ cup seedless red raspberry jam
3 cups semisweet chocolate chips
½ cup vegetable shortening plus additional for greasing

1. Preheat oven to 350°F. Grease and flour 13×9×2-inch pan.

2. Prepare, bake and cool cake following package directions for basic recipe.
Remove from pan. Cover and store overnight (see Tip). Level top of cake.
Trim ¼-inch strip of cake from all sides. (Be careful to make straight cuts.)
Cut cake into small squares, rectangles or triangles with serrated knife. Cut
round and heart shapes with 1½- to 2-inch cookie cutters. Split each
individual cake horizontally into two layers.

3. For filling, cut almond paste in half. Roll half the paste between two
sheets of waxed paper to ⅛-inch thickness. Cut into same shapes as
individual cakes. Repeat with second half of paste. Warm jam in small
saucepan over low heat until thin. Remove top of one cake. Spread ¼ to
½ teaspoon jam on inside of each cut surface. Place one almond paste cutout
on bottom layer. Top with second half of cake, jam side down. Repeat with
remaining cakes.

4. For glaze, place chocolate chips and ½ cup shortening in 4-cup glass
measuring cup. Microwave at MEDIUM (50% power) for 2 minutes; stir.
Microwave for 2 minutes longer at MEDIUM; stir until smooth. Place
3 assembled cakes on cooling rack over bowl. Spoon chocolate glaze over
each cake until top and sides are completely covered. Remove to waxed
paper when glaze has stopped dripping. Repeat process until all cakes are
covered. (Return chocolate glaze in bowl to glass measuring cup as needed;
microwave at MEDIUM for 30 to 60 seconds to thin.)

5. Place remaining chocolate glaze in resealable plastic bag; seal. Place bag
in bowl of hot water for several minutes. Dry with paper towel. Knead until
chocolate is smooth. Snip pinpoint hole in bottom corner of bag. Drizzle or
decorate top of each petit four. Let stand until chocolate is set. Store in
single layer in airtight containers.   *Makes 24 to 32 servings*

Tip: To make cutting the cake into shapes easier, bake the cake one day
before assembling.

Chocolate Petits Fours

Heavenly Chocolate Mousse Pie

4 (1-ounce) squares unsweetened chocolate, melted
1 (14-ounce) can EAGLE BRAND® Sweetened Condensed Milk
(NOT evaporated milk)
1½ teaspoons vanilla extract
1 cup (½ pint) whipping cream, whipped
1 (8-inch) prepared chocolate or graham cracker crumb crust

1. In medium bowl, beat melted chocolate with EAGLE BRAND® and vanilla until well blended. Chill 15 minutes or until cooled; stir until smooth. Fold in whipped cream.

2. Pour into crust. Chill thoroughly. Garnish as desired. Store leftovers covered in refrigerator. *Makes 1 (8-inch) pie*

Prep Time: 20 minutes
Chill Time: 15 minutes

Cocoa Cappuccino Mousse

1 can (14 ounces) sweetened condensed milk (not evaporated milk)
⅓ cup HERSHEY'S Cocoa
3 tablespoons butter or margarine
2 teaspoons powdered instant coffee or espresso, dissolved in
2 teaspoons hot water
2 cups (1 pint) cold whipping cream

1. Combine sweetened condensed milk, cocoa, butter and coffee in medium saucepan. Cook over low heat, stirring constantly, until butter melts and mixture is smooth. Remove from heat; cool.

2. Beat whipping cream in large bowl until stiff. Gradually fold chocolate mixture into whipped cream. Spoon into dessert dishes. Refrigerate until set, about 2 hours. Garnish as desired. *Makes 8 servings*

Prep Time: 15 minutes
Cook Time: 10 minutes
Chill Time: 2 hours

Heavenly Chocolate Mousse Pie

Cookies and Cream Cheesecake Bonbons

24 chocolate creme-filled sandwich cookies, divided
1 package (8 ounces) cream cheese, softened
1 cup nonfat dry milk powder
1 teaspoon vanilla
1 package (1 pound) powdered sugar (about 4 cups)

1. Coarsely chop 12 cookies. Place remaining 12 cookies in food processor; process until fine crumbs form. Place crumbs on baking sheet lined with waxed paper; set aside.

2. Beat cream cheese, dry milk powder and vanilla in large bowl with electric mixer at medium speed until smooth. Beat in powdered sugar, 1 cup at a time, at low speed until mixture is smooth. Stir in reserved chopped cookies. Refrigerate 2 hours or until firm.

3. Shape rounded tablespoonfuls cream cheese mixture into balls. Roll balls in reserved cookie crumbs. Store in airtight container in refrigerator.

Makes about 3 dozen bonbons

Chocolate Croissant Pudding

1½ cups milk
 3 eggs
½ cup sugar
¼ cup unsweetened cocoa powder
½ teaspoon vanilla
¼ teaspoon salt
 2 plain croissants, cut into 1-inch pieces
½ cup chocolate chips
   Whipped cream

Slow Cooker Directions
1. Grease 1-quart casserole. Beat milk, eggs, sugar, cocoa, vanilla and salt in medium bowl. Layer half of croissants, chocolate chips and half of egg mixture in prepared casserole. Top with remaining croissants and egg mixture.

2. Add rack to 5-quart slow cooker; pour in 1 cup water. Place casserole on rack. Cover; cook on LOW 3 to 4 hours. Remove casserole from slow cooker. Serve with whipped cream.

Makes 6 servings

Cookies and Cream Cheesecake Bonbons

Two Great Tastes Pudding Parfaits

1 package (6-serving size, 4.6 ounces) vanilla cook & serve pudding and pie filling mix*
3½ cups milk
1 cup REESE'S® Peanut Butter Chips
1 cup HERSHEY¿S MINI KISSES® Brand Milk Chocolates
Whipped topping (optional)
Additional MINI KISSES® Brand Milk Chocolates or grated chocolate

*Do not use instant pudding mix.

1. Combine pudding mix and 3½ cups milk in large heavy saucepan (rather than amount listed in package directions). Cook over medium heat, stirring constantly, until mixture comes to a full boil. Remove from heat; divide hot mixture between 2 heatproof medium bowls.

2. Immediately stir peanut butter chips into mixture in one bowl and chocolates into second bowl. Stir both mixtures until chips are melted and mixture is smooth. Cool slightly, stirring occasionally.

3. Alternately layer peanut butter and chocolate mixtures in parfait dishes, wine glasses or dessert dishes. Place plastic wrap directly onto surface of each dessert; refrigerate about 6 hours. Garnish with whipped topping, if desired, and chocolate pieces.   *Makes 4 to 6 servings*

White Chocolate Mousse

1 cup vanilla milk chips *or* 7 ounces white chocolate, chopped
¼ cup hot water
2 teaspoons WATKINS® Vanilla
2 cups heavy whipping cream
½ cup sifted powdered sugar

Melt vanilla chips in top of double boiler or in microwave oven. Add hot water and vanilla; mix until smooth. Cool completely. Beat cream until it begins to thicken. Add sugar; continue beating until soft peaks form. Stir large spoonful of whipped cream into vanilla chip mixture, then fold mixture back into remaining whipped cream. Spoon mousse into individual custard cups or 4-cup mold. Refrigerate until thoroughly chilled. Serve cold.

Makes 8 servings

Chocolate Banana Split Pie

32 chocolate wafer cookies
16 vanilla wafer cookies
6 tablespoons margarine, melted
1 cup sugar
⅓ cup unsweetened cocoa powder
¼ cup cornstarch
2½ tablespoons flour
¼ teaspoon salt
2½ cups milk
2 egg yolks, lightly beaten
2 tablespoons margarine
1 teaspoon vanilla extract
2 firm DOLE® Bananas

• Place cookies in food processor container or blender. Cover; process until fine. Combine with margarine until mixed. Press on bottom and up side of greased 9-inch pie plate. Bake at 375°F 5 minutes. Cool.

• Combine sugar, cocoa, cornstarch, flour and salt in saucepan. Stir in milk and egg yolks until blended. Cook over low heat, stirring, until mixture boils and thickens. Remove from heat. Stir in margarine and vanilla.

• Pour chocolate mixture into bowl. Cover surface with plastic wrap. Refrigerate 15 minutes.

• Spread half of filling into prepared crust. Slice bananas; arrange slices over filling. Cover with remaining filling. Press plastic wrap on surface. Refrigerate 4 hours. Remove plastic wrap. Garnish with sliced strawberries, if desired. *Makes 8 servings*

Prep Time: 25 minutes
Chill Time: 4 hours

Rich Chocolate Mousse

1 cup (6 ounces) NESTLÉ® TOLL HOUSE® Semi-Sweet Chocolate
   Morsels
3 tablespoons butter, cut into pieces
2 teaspoons TASTER'S CHOICE® 100% Pure Instant Coffee
1 tablespoon hot water
2 teaspoons vanilla extract
½ cup heavy whipping cream

MICROWAVE morsels and butter in medium, uncovered, microwave-safe
bowl on HIGH (100%) power for 1 minute. STIR. Morsels may retain
some of their original shape. If necessary, microwave at additional 10- to
15-second intervals, stirring just until morsels are melted. Dissolve Taster's
Choice in hot water; stir into chocolate. Stir in vanilla extract; cool to room
temperature.

WHIP cream in small mixer bowl on high speed until stiff peaks form; fold
into chocolate mixture. Spoon into tall glasses; refrigerate for 1 hour or until
set. Garnish as desired. *Makes 2 servings*

Chocolate Pudding

1 (14-ounce) can EAGLE BRAND® Sweetened Condensed Milk
   (NOT evaporated milk)
2 cups water, divided
¼ teaspoon salt
3 (1-ounce) squares unsweetened chocolate
3 tablespoons cornstarch
1 teaspoon vanilla extract

1. In top of double boiler, combine EAGLE BRAND®, 1½ cups water
and salt. Add chocolate. Cook over hot water, stirring until chocolate melts.
Gradually stir remaining ½ cup water into cornstarch, keeping mixture
smooth. Gradually add to milk mixture; stir rapidly. Continue to cook,
stirring constantly until thickened. Stir in vanilla.

2. Divide pudding evenly among six individual dessert dishes. Refrigerate.
Makes 6 (½-cup) servings

Rich Chocolate Mousse

Cookies 'n' Crème Fudge

3 (6-ounce) packages white chocolate baking squares
1 (14-ounce) can EAGLE BRAND® Sweetened Condensed Milk (NOT evaporated milk)
⅛ teaspoon salt
2 cups coarsely crushed chocolate crème-filled sandwich cookies (about 20 cookies)

1. Line 8-inch square baking pan with waxed paper. In heavy saucepan over low heat, melt white chocolate with EAGLE BRAND® and salt. Remove from heat. Stir in crushed cookies. Spread evenly in prepared pan. Chill 2 hours or until firm.

2. Turn fudge onto cutting board. Peel off paper; cut into squares. Store tightly covered at room temperature.   *Makes about 2½ pounds fudge*

Prep Time: 10 minutes
Chill Time: 2 hours

Chocolate Triple Layer Pie

2 cups cold milk
2 (4-serving-size) packages chocolate flavor instant pudding & pie filling
1 (6-ounce) READY CRUST® Graham Cracker Pie Crust
1 (8-ounce) tub frozen whipped topping, thawed, divided

1. Pour milk into large bowl. Add pudding mixes. Beat with wire whisk 1 minute. (Mixture will be thick.) Spoon 1½ cups of pudding into crust.

2. Gently stir half of whipped topping into remaining pudding. Spread over pudding in crust. Top with remaining whipped topping.

3. Refrigerate 4 hours or until set. Refrigerate leftovers.

Makes 8 servings

Prep Time: 15 minutes
Chill Time: 4 hours

Cookies 'n' Crème Fudge

Nestlé® Toll House® Chocolate Chip Pie

1 *unbaked* 9-inch (4-cup volume) deep-dish pie shell*
2 large eggs
½ cup all-purpose flour
½ cup granulated sugar
½ cup packed brown sugar
¾ cup (1½ sticks) butter, softened
1 cup (6 ounces) NESTLÉ® TOLL HOUSE® Semi-Sweet
    Chocolate Morsels
1 cup chopped nuts
    Sweetened whipped cream or ice cream (optional)

If using frozen pie shell, use deep-dish style, thawed completely. Bake on baking sheet; increase baking time slightly.

PREHEAT oven to 325°F.

BEAT eggs in large mixer bowl on high speed until foamy. Beat in flour, granulated sugar and brown sugar. Beat in butter. Stir in morsels and nuts. Spoon into pie shell.

BAKE for 55 to 60 minutes or until knife inserted halfway between outside edge and center comes out clean. Cool on wire rack. Serve warm with whipped cream. *Makes 8 servings*

Nestlé® Toll House® Chocolate Chip Pie

Quick Chocolate Fixes

Chocolate Peanut Butter Candy Bars

1 package (18¼ ounces) devil's food or dark chocolate cake mix
without pudding in the mix
1 can (5 ounces) evaporated milk
⅓ cup butter, melted
½ cup dry-roasted peanuts
4 packages (1½ ounces each) chocolate peanut butter cups, coarsely
chopped

1. Preheat oven to 350°F. Lightly grease 13×9-inch baking pan. Beat cake mix, evaporated milk and butter in large bowl with electric mixer at medium speed until well blended. (Dough will be stiff.) Spread two thirds of dough in prepared pan. Sprinkle with peanuts.

2. Bake 10 minutes; remove from oven and sprinkle with chopped candy. Drop remaining dough by large spoonfuls over candy. Bake 15 to 20 minutes or until set. Cool completely on wire rack.   *Makes 2 dozen bars*

Clockwise from top left: *Chocolate Peanut Butter Candy Bars, Frozen Chocolate-Covered Bananas (page 124), Milk Chocolate Pots de Crème (page 116) and Luscious Chocolate Covered Strawberries (page 124)*

Mini Chocolate Pies

1 package (4-serving size) vanilla cook & serve pudding and pie
   filling mix*
1 cup HERSHEY'S MINI CHIPS™ Semi-Sweet Chocolate Chips
1 package (4 ounces) single serve graham cracker crusts (6 crusts)
   Whipped topping
   Additional HERSHEY'S MINI CHIPS™ Semi-Sweet Chocolate
   Chips

Do not use instant pudding mix.

1. Prepare pudding and pie filling mix as directed on package; remove from heat. Immediately add 1 cup small chocolate chips; stir until melted. Cool 5 minutes, stirring occasionally.

2. Pour filling into crusts; press plastic wrap directly onto surface. Refrigerate several hours or until firm. Garnish with whipped topping and small chocolate chips. *Makes 6 servings*

Prep Time: 5 minutes
Cook Time: 10 minutes
Cool Time: 5 minutes
Chill Time: 2 hours

Raisin Clusters

1 cup milk chocolate chips
⅓ cup sweetened condensed milk
1 teaspoon vanilla
2 cups raisins

1. Line baking sheet with buttered waxed paper. Heat chocolate chips, condensed milk and vanilla in heavy small saucepan over low heat, stirring occasionally, until melted and smooth. Remove from heat; stir in raisins.

2. Drop by teaspoonfuls onto prepared baking sheet. Refrigerate until firm. Store in refrigerator in airtight container between layers of waxed paper.
Makes 30 clusters

Mini Chocolate Pies

Festive Fudge

3 cups (18 ounces) semi-sweet chocolate chips (or milk chocolate chips)
1 (14-ounce) can EAGLE BRAND® Sweetened Condensed Milk
   (NOT evaporated milk)
  Dash salt
½ to 1 cup chopped nuts (optional)
1½ teaspoons vanilla extract

1. Line 8- or 9-inch square pan with foil, extending foil over edges of pan. Butter foil; set aside. In heavy saucepan over low heat, melt chips with EAGLE BRAND® and salt. Remove from heat; stir in nuts, if desired, and vanilla. Spread evenly into prepared pan.

2. Chill 2 hours or until firm. Turn fudge onto cutting board, peel off paper and cut into squares. Store covered in refrigerator.

Makes about 2 pounds

Chocolate Peanut Butter Chip Glazed Fudge: Proceed as above, substituting ¾ cup peanut butter chips in place of nuts. To make the glaze, melt ½ cup peanut butter chips with ½ cup whipping cream; stir until thick and smooth. Spread over fudge.

Marshmallow Fudge: Proceed as above, omitting nuts and adding 2 tablespoons butter to mixture. Fold in 2 cups miniature marshmallows.

Gift Tips: Create delicious homemade gifts from an assortment of flavored fudges, packed in decorative tins, candy bags or boxes. Wrap individual pieces of fudge in colored food-grade cellophane, candy wrappers or gold or silver foil candy cups, and arrange in gift bags or tins. Store in refrigerator.

Festive Fudge, Chocolate Peanut Butter Chip
Glazed Fudge and Marshmallow Fudge

Milk Chocolate Pots de Crème

2 cups (11½-ounce package) HERSHEY'S Milk Chocolate Chips
½ cup light cream
½ teaspoon vanilla extract
   Sweetened whipped cream (optional)

1. Place milk chocolate chips and light cream in medium microwave-safe bowl. Microwave on HIGH (100%) 1 minute or just until chips are melted and mixture is smooth when stirred. Stir in vanilla.

2. Pour into demitasse cups or very small dessert dishes. Cover; refrigerate until firm. Serve cold with sweetened whipped cream, if desired.

Makes 6 to 8 servings

Creamy Hot Chocolate

1 (14-ounce) can EAGLE BRAND® Sweetened Condensed Milk
   (NOT evaporated milk)
½ cup unsweetened cocoa
1½ teaspoons vanilla extract
⅛ teaspoon salt
6½ cups hot water
   Marshmallows (optional)

1. In large saucepan over medium heat, combine EAGLE BRAND®, cocoa, vanilla and salt; mix well.

2. Slowly stir in water. Heat through, stirring occasionally. Do not boil. Top with marshmallows, if desired. Store covered in refrigerator.

Makes about 2 quarts

Microwave Directions: In 2-quart glass measure, combine all ingredients except marshmallows. Microwave at HIGH (100% power) 8 to 10 minutes, stirring every 3 minutes. Top with marshmallows, if desired. Store covered in refrigerator.

Tip: Hot chocolate can be stored in the refrigerator for up to 5 days. Mix well and reheat before serving.

Prep Time: 8 to 10 minutes

Ultimate Chocolate Dip

⅔ cup KARO® Light Corn Syrup
½ cup heavy cream
1 (8-ounce) package semisweet chocolate or 1½ cups semisweet
    chocolate chips
Fresh fruit, marshmallows, brownies or cookies (optional)

1. In medium saucepan combine corn syrup and cream. Bring to a boil over medium heat. Remove from heat; add chocolate and stir until melted.

2. Serve warm with fruit, marshmallows, brownies or cookies, as desired.

Makes 2 cups

Microwave Directions: In medium microwavable bowl stir corn syrup and cream. Microwave on High (100%) 1½ minutes or until boiling. Add chocolate; stir until melted.

Prep Time: 5 minutes
Cook Time: 10 minutes

Chocolate Peanut Butter Pie

1 can (14 ounces) sweetened condensed milk
¼ cup creamy peanut butter
2 tablespoons unsweetened cocoa powder
1 container (8 ounces) nondairy frozen whipped topping, thawed
1 (6-ounce) chocolate cookie crumb crust

1. Beat sweetened condensed milk, peanut butter and cocoa in large bowl with electric mixer until smooth and well blended. Fold in whipped topping. Pour mixture into crust.

2. Freeze at least 6 hours or overnight. Garnish as desired.

Makes 8 servings

German Chocolate No-Cook Fudge

3 packages (4 ounces each) German sweet chocolate, broken into
    pieces
1 cup (6 ounces) semisweet chocolate chips
1 can (14 ounces) sweetened condensed milk
1 cup chopped pecans
2 teaspoons vanilla
36 pecan halves (optional)

1. Butter 8-inch square pan. Place chocolate and chips in microwavable
bowl. Microwave on HIGH 1 minute; stir. Microwave for 30-second
intervals, stirring after each interval, until mixture is melted and smooth.

2. Add sweetened condensed milk, chopped pecans and vanilla; stir until
well blended. Spread in prepared pan. Score fudge into squares with knife.
Place pecan half on each square, if desired. Refrigerate until firm.

3. Cut fudge into squares along score marks. Store in refrigerator. Bring to
room temperature before serving.   *Makes about 2 pounds fudge*

Choco-Hot Sauce

1 cup semisweet chocolate chips
⅓ cup sugar
⅓ cup water
2 tablespoons butter
1½ teaspoons TABASCO® brand Pepper Sauce

Combine chocolate chips, sugar, water and butter in small saucepan over
medium heat; heat just to boiling, stirring constantly. Remove from heat;
stir in TABASCO® Sauce. Serve warm over ice cream, cake or fruit.

Makes 1 cup sauce

German Chocolate No-Cook Fudge

Rocky Road Candy

1 (12-ounce) package semi-sweet chocolate chips
2 tablespoons butter or margarine
1 (14-ounce) can EAGLE BRAND® Sweetened Condensed Milk
   (NOT evaporated milk)
2 cups dry roasted peanuts
1 (10½-ounce) package miniature marshmallows

1. Line 13×9-inch baking pan with waxed paper. In heavy saucepan over low heat, melt chips and butter with EAGLE BRAND®; remove from heat.

2. In large bowl, combine peanuts and marshmallows; stir in chocolate mixture. Spread in prepared pan. Chill 2 hours or until firm.

3. Remove candy from pan; peel off paper and cut into squares. Store loosely covered at room temperature. *Makes about 3½ dozen candies*

Microwave Directions: In 1-quart glass measure, combine chips, butter and EAGLE BRAND®. Microwave at HIGH (100% power) 3 minutes, stirring after 1½ minutes. Stir to melt chips. Let stand 5 minutes. Proceed as directed above.

Prep Time: 10 minutes
Chill Time: 2 hours

Passion Truffles

6 squares (1 ounce each) bittersweet or semi-sweet chocolate
¼ cup I CAN'T BELIEVE IT'S NOT BUTTER!® Spread
2 tablespoons coffee liqueur or brandy (optional)
   Ground nuts, confectioners sugar or unsweetened cocoa powder

In medium microwave-safe bowl, microwave chocolate and I Can't Believe It's Not Butter!® Spread at HIGH (100%) 1 minute or until chocolate is melted; stir until smooth. Stir in liqueur. Refrigerate 1 hour or until firm.

Scoop chocolate mixture by level tablespoonfuls and roll into balls. Roll in nuts, sugar or cocoa powder. Store in airtight container in cool place, or refrigerate or freeze up to 2 weeks. *Makes 16 truffles*

Rocky Road Candy

120

Spanish Chocolate

2 cups (1 pint) light cream or half-and-half
4 HERSHEY'S Milk Chocolate Bars (1.55 ounces *each*), broken into
  pieces
¼ cup brewed coffee *or* ½ teaspoon powdered instant coffee dissolved
  in ¼ cup boiling water
Whipped cream (optional)
Crushed ice (optional)

Combine light cream and chocolate in medium saucepan. Cook over low
heat, stirring constantly, until chocolate is melted and mixture is smooth.
Stir in coffee. Beat with rotary beater or whisk until foamy. Serve hot
with whipped cream, or cool and serve over crushed ice, if desired.

Makes 5 servings

Fudgy Banana Rocky Road Clusters

1 package (12 ounces) semisweet chocolate chips
⅓ cup peanut butter
3 cups miniature marshmallows
1 cup unsalted peanuts
1 cup banana chips

Line baking sheets with waxed paper; grease waxed paper. Place chocolate
chips and peanut butter in large microwavable bowl. Microwave on HIGH
2 minutes or until chips are melted and mixture is smooth, stirring twice.
Fold in marshmallows, peanuts and banana chips.

Drop rounded tablespoonfuls of candy mixture onto prepared baking sheets;
refrigerate until firm. Store in airtight container in refrigerator.

Makes 2½ to 3 dozen clusters

Hot Fudge Sauce

1 cup (6 ounces) semi-sweet chocolate chips *or* 4 (1-ounce) squares
    semi-sweet chocolate
2 tablespoons butter or margarine
1 (14-ounce) can EAGLE BRAND® Sweetened Condensed Milk
    (NOT evaporated milk)
2 tablespoons water
1 teaspoon vanilla extract

1. In heavy saucepan over medium heat, melt chips and butter with EAGLE BRAND® and water. Cook and stir constantly until smooth. Stir in vanilla.

2. Serve warm over ice cream or as dipping sauce for fruit. Store leftovers covered in refrigerator.   *Makes 2 cups sauce*

Microwave Directions: In 1-quart glass measure, combine ingredients. Microwave at HIGH (100% power) 3 to 3½ minutes, stirring after each minute. Proceed as directed above.

To Reheat: In small heavy saucepan, combine desired amount of Hot Fudge Sauce with small amount of water. Over low heat, stir constantly until heated through.

Spirited Hot Fudge Sauce: Add ¼ cup almond, coffee, mint or orange-flavored liqueur with vanilla.

Prep Time: 10 minutes

Frozen Chocolate-Covered Bananas

2 ripe medium bananas
4 wooden sticks
½ cup granola cereal without raisins
⅓ cup hot fudge topping, at room temperature

1. Line baking sheet or 15×10-inch jelly-roll pan with waxed paper. Peel bananas; cut in half crosswise. Insert wooden stick into center of cut end of each banana half about 1½ inches into banana. Place on prepared baking sheet; freeze until firm, at least 2 hours.

2. Place granola in large plastic food storage bag; crush slightly using rolling pin. Transfer to shallow plate. Place hot fudge topping in shallow dish.

3. Working with one banana at a time, place frozen banana in fudge topping; turn and spread topping evenly over banana. Immediately place banana on plate with granola; turn to coat lightly. Return to baking sheet in freezer. Repeat with remaining bananas. Freeze until hot fudge topping is very firm, at least 2 hours. Let stand 5 minutes before serving.   *Makes 4 servings*

Luscious Chocolate Covered Strawberries

3 squares (1 ounce each) semi-sweet chocolate
2 tablespoons I CAN'T BELIEVE IT'S NOT BUTTER!® Spread
1 tablespoon coffee liqueur (optional)
6 to 8 large strawberries with stems

In small microwave-safe bowl, microwave chocolate and I Can't Believe It's Not Butter!® Spread at HIGH (100%) 1 minute or until chocolate is melted; stir until smooth. Stir in liqueur. Dip strawberries in chocolate mixture, then refrigerate on waxed paper-lined baking sheet until chocolate is set, at least 1 hour.   *Makes 6 to 8 strawberries*

Frozen Chocolate-Covered Bananas

Special Dark® Fudge Fondue

2 cups (12-ounce package) HERSHEY'S SPECIAL DARK®
  Chocolate Chips
½ cup light cream
2 teaspoons vanilla extract
  Assorted fondue dippers such as marshmallows, cherries, grapes,
  mandarin orange segments, pineapple chunks, strawberries,
  slices of other fresh fruits, small pieces of cake or small brownies

1. Place chocolate chips and light cream in medium microwave-safe bowl. Microwave on HIGH (100%) 1 minute or just until chips are melted and mixture is smooth when stirred. Stir in vanilla.

2. Pour into fondue pot or chafing dish; serve warm with fondue dippers. If mixture thickens, stir in additional light cream, one tablespoon at a time. Refrigerate leftover fondue.   *Makes 1½ cups fondue*

Stovetop Directions:
Combine chocolate chips and light cream in heavy medium saucepan. Cook over low heat, stirring constantly, until chips are melted and mixture is hot. Stir in vanilla and continue as in Step 2 above.

Peanutty Chocolate Sauce

½ cup KARO® Light or Dark Corn Syrup
½ cup creamy or chunk peanut butter
¼ cup heavy cream or evaporated milk
½ cup (3 ounces) semisweet chocolate chips

1. In 1½-quart microwavable bowl, combine corn syrup, peanut butter and cream.

2. Microwave on HIGH (100%) 1½ minutes or until boiling. Add chocolate; stir until melted.

3. Serve warm over ice cream. Refrigerate in tightly covered container.
Makes about 1¼ cups

Special Dark® Fudge Fondue

Hot Cocoa

½ **cup sugar**
¼ **cup HERSHEY₂S Cocoa**
   Dash salt
⅓ **cup hot water**
 4 cups (1 quart) milk
¾ **teaspoon vanilla extract**
   Miniature marshmallows *or* sweetened whipped cream (optional)

1. Stir together sugar, cocoa and salt in medium saucepan; stir in water. Cook over medium heat, stirring constantly, until mixture comes to a boil. Boil 2 minutes, stirring constantly. Add milk; heat to serving temperature, stirring constantly. *Do not boil.*

2. Remove from heat; add vanilla. Beat with rotary beater or whisk until foamy. Serve topped with marshmallows or sweetened whipped cream, if desired.   *Makes 5 (8-ounce) servings*

Spiced Cocoa: Add ⅛ teaspoon ground cinnamon and ⅛ teaspoon ground nutmeg with vanilla. Serve with cinnamon stick, if desired.

Mint Cocoa: Add ½ teaspoon mint extract *or* 3 tablespoons crushed hard peppermint candy *or* 2 to 3 tablespoons white crème de menthe with vanilla. Serve with peppermint candy stick, if desired.

Citrus Cocoa: Add ½ teaspoon orange extract *or* 2 to 3 tablespoons orange liqueur with vanilla.

Swiss Mocha: Add 2 to 2½ teaspoons powdered instant coffee with vanilla.

Canadian Cocoa: Add ½ teaspoon maple extract with vanilla.

Cocoa Au Lait: Omit marshmallows or sweetened whipped cream. Spoon 2 tablespoons softened vanilla ice cream on top of each cup of cocoa at serving time.

Quick Microwave Cocoa: To make one serving, in microwave-safe cup or mug, combine 1 heaping teaspoon HERSHEY₂S Cocoa, 2 heaping teaspoons sugar and dash of salt. Add 2 teaspoons cold milk; stir until smooth. Fill cup with milk. Microwave on HIGH (100%) 1 to 1½ minutes or until hot. Stir to blend.

Quick Chocolate Mousse

1 (14-ounce) can EAGLE BRAND® Sweetened Condensed Milk
(NOT evaporated milk)
1 (4-serving-size) package instant chocolate pudding and pie filling
mix
1 cup cold water
1 cup (½ pint) whipping cream, whipped

1. In large bowl, beat EAGLE BRAND®, pudding mix and water; chill
5 minutes.

2. Fold in whipped cream. Spoon into serving dishes; chill. Garnish as
desired.   *Makes 8 to 10 servings*

Prep Time: 5 minutes

No-Bake Chocolate
Peanut Butter Balls

2 cups honey nut creamy or chunky peanut butter
2 cups graham cracker crumbs
1 cup confectioners' sugar
½ cup KARO® Light or Dark Corn Syrup
1 cup semisweet chocolate chips, melted

1. In large bowl, stir peanut butter, graham cracker crumbs, confectioners'
sugar and corn syrup until smooth.

2. Shape into 1-inch balls. Place on waxed paper-lined cookie sheet.

3. Drizzle melted chocolate over balls or dip balls in melted chocolate. Chill
for 30 minutes to set chocolate.   *Makes 6 dozen*

Prep Time: 30 minutes
Chill Time: 30 minutes

Chocolate For Breakfast

Toll House® Mini Morsel Pancakes

2½ cups all-purpose flour
  1 cup (6 ounces) NESTLÉ® TOLL HOUSE® Semi-Sweet Chocolate
    Mini Morsels
  1 tablespoon baking powder
  ½ teaspoon salt
1¾ cups milk
  2 large eggs
  ⅓ cup vegetable oil
  ⅓ cup packed brown sugar
    Powdered sugar, fresh sliced strawberries and maple syrup

COMBINE flour, morsels, baking powder and salt in large bowl. Combine milk, eggs, vegetable oil and brown sugar in medium bowl; add to flour mixture. Stir just until moistened (batter may be lumpy).

HEAT griddle or skillet over medium heat; brush lightly with vegetable oil. Pour *¼ cup* of batter onto hot griddle; cook until bubbles begin to burst. Turn; continue to cook for about 1 minute longer or until golden. Repeat with *remaining* batter.

SPRINKLE with powdered sugar; top with strawberries. Serve with maple syrup. *Makes about 18 pancakes*

Clockwise from top left: Peanut Butter Mini Muffins (page 148), Toll House® Mini Morsel Pancakes, Lots o' Chocolate Bread (page 143) and Chocolate Chip Coffeecake (page 136)

Mocha-Macadamia Nut Muffins

1¼ cups all-purpose flour
⅔ cup granulated sugar
2½ tablespoons unsweetened cocoa powder
1 teaspoon baking soda
¼ teaspoon salt
⅔ cup buttermilk*
3 tablespoons butter, melted
1 egg, beaten
1 tablespoon instant coffee granules dissolved in 1 tablespoon
    hot water
¾ teaspoon vanilla
½ cup coarsely chopped macadamia nuts
    Powdered sugar (optional)

Soured fresh milk can be substituted for buttermilk. To sour milk, combine 2 teaspoons lemon juice plus enough milk to equal ⅔ cup. Stir; let stand 5 minutes before using.

1. Preheat oven to 400°F. Lightly grease 12 standard (2½-inch) muffin pan cups or line with paper baking cups.

2. Combine flour, granulated sugar, cocoa, baking soda and salt in large bowl. Combine buttermilk, butter, egg, coffee mixture and vanilla in medium bowl; beat until blended. Stir buttermilk mixture into flour mixture just until dry ingredients are moistened. Stir in macadamia nuts. Spoon batter evenly into prepared muffin cups.

3. Bake 13 to 17 minutes or until toothpick inserted into centers comes out clean. Cool in pan on wire rack 5 minutes. Remove from pan; cool on wire rack 10 minutes. Sprinkle with powdered sugar, if desired.

Makes 12 muffins

Mocha-Macadamia Nut Muffins

Petit Pain au Chocolate

1 package (17.25 ounces) frozen puff pastry sheets, thawed
1 cup (6 ounces) NESTLÉ® TOLL HOUSE® Milk Chocolate Morsels,
  divided
1 large egg, beaten
1 bar (2 ounces *total*) NESTLÉ® TOLL HOUSE® Semi-Sweet
  Chocolate Baking Bars, broken into pieces
2 tablespoons butter or margarine
1 cup powdered sugar
2 tablespoons hot water

PREHEAT oven to 350°F. Grease 2 baking sheets.

UNFOLD *1* pastry sheet on lightly floured surface. Roll out to make 10-inch square. Cut into 4 squares. Place *2 tablespoons* morsels in center of each square. Brush edges lightly with beaten egg and fold squares to form triangles. Press edges to seal. Place on prepared baking sheet about 2 inches apart. Repeat with *remaining* pastry sheet. Brush top of each pastry with beaten egg.

BAKE for 15 to 17 minutes or until puffed and golden. Cool on baking sheets for 2 minutes; remove to wire racks to cool completely.

MELT baking bar and butter in small, uncovered, microwave-safe bowl on HIGH (100%) power for 30 seconds. STIR. Bar may retain some of its original shape. If necessary, microwave at additional 10- to 15-second intervals, stirring just until bar is melted. Stir in sugar. Add water, stirring until icing is smooth, adding additional water if necessary. Drizzle icing over pastries. *Makes 8 pastries*

Petit Pain au Chocolate

Chocolate Chip Coffeecake

3 cups all-purpose flour, divided
⅓ cup sugar
2 envelopes FLEISCHMANN'S® RapidRise™ Yeast
1 teaspoon salt
½ cup milk
½ cup water
½ cup (1 stick) butter or margarine
2 large eggs
¾ cup semi-sweet chocolate morsels
    Chocolate Nut Topping (recipe follows)

In large bowl, combine 1 cup flour, sugar, undissolved yeast and salt. Heat milk, water and butter until very warm (120° to 130°F). Gradually add to dry ingredients. Beat 2 minutes at medium speed of electric mixer, scraping bowl occasionally. Add eggs and 1 cup flour; beat 2 minutes at high speed, scraping bowl occasionally. Stir in chocolate morsels and remaining flour to make soft batter. Turn into greased 13×9×2-inch baking pan. Cover; let rise in warm, draft-free place until doubled in size, about 1 hour.

Bake at 400°F for 15 minutes; remove from oven and sprinkle with Chocolate Nut Topping. Return to oven and bake additional 10 minutes or until done. Cool in pan for 10 minutes. Remove from pan; cool on wire rack.   *Makes 1 cake*

Chocolate Nut Topping: In medium bowl, cut ½ cup butter into ⅔ cup all-purpose flour until crumbly. Stir in ⅔ cup sugar, 2 teaspoons ground cinnamon, 1 cup semi-sweet chocolate morsels and 1 cup chopped pecans.

Double Chocolate Zucchini Muffins

2⅓ cups all-purpose flour
1¼ cups sugar
 ⅓ cup unsweetened cocoa powder
 2 teaspoons baking powder
1½ teaspoons ground cinnamon
 1 teaspoon baking soda
 ½ teaspoon salt
 1 cup sour cream
 ½ cup vegetable oil
 2 eggs, beaten
 ¼ cup milk
 1 cup milk chocolate chips
 1 cup shredded zucchini

1. Preheat oven to 400°F. Grease 12 (3½-inch) large muffin pan cups.

2. Combine flour, sugar, cocoa, baking powder, cinnamon, baking soda and salt in large bowl. Combine sour cream, oil, eggs and milk in small bowl until blended; stir into flour mixture just until moistened. Fold in chocolate chips and zucchini. Spoon into prepared muffin cups, filling half full.

3. Bake 25 to 30 minutes or until toothpick inserted into centers comes out clean. Cool in pan on wire rack 5 minutes. Remove from pan; cool completely on wire rack. Store covered at room temperature.

Makes 12 jumbo muffins

Fudgey Peanut Butter Chip Muffins

½ cup applesauce
½ cup quick-cooking rolled oats
¼ cup (½ stick) butter or margarine, softened
½ cup granulated sugar
½ cup packed light brown sugar
 1 egg
½ teaspoon vanilla extract
¾ cup all-purpose flour
¼ cup HERSHEY'S SPECIAL DARK® Cocoa or HERSHEY'S
 Cocoa
½ teaspoon baking soda
¼ teaspoon ground cinnamon (optional)
 1 cup REESE'S® Peanut Butter Chips
 Powdered sugar (optional)

1. Heat oven to 350°F. Line muffin cups (2½ inches in diameter) with paper baking cups.

2. Stir together applesauce and oats in small bowl; set aside. Beat butter, granulated sugar, brown sugar, egg and vanilla in large bowl until well blended. Add applesauce mixture; blend well. Stir together flour, cocoa, baking soda and cinnamon, if desired. Add to butter mixture, blending well. Stir in peanut butter chips. Fill muffin cups ¾ full with batter.

3. Bake 22 to 26 minutes or until wooden pick inserted in center comes out almost clean. Cool slightly in pan on wire rack. Sprinkle muffin tops with powdered sugar, if desired. Serve warm.   *Makes 12 to 15 muffins*

Fudgey Chocolate Chip Muffins: Omit Peanut Butter Chips. Add 1 cup HERSHEY'S Semi-Sweet Chocolate Chips.

Fudgey Peanut Butter Chip Muffins

Whip 'em Up Wacky Waffles

1½ cups biscuit baking mix
1 cup buttermilk
1 large egg
1 tablespoon vegetable oil
½ cup "M&M's"® Semi-Sweet Chocolate Mini Baking Bits
Powdered sugar and maple syrup

Preheat Belgian waffle iron. In large bowl combine baking mix, buttermilk, egg and oil until well mixed. Spoon about ½ cup batter into hot waffle iron. Sprinkle with about 2 tablespoons "M&M's"® Semi-Sweet Chocolate Mini Baking Bits; top with about ½ cup batter. Close lid and bake until steaming stops, 1 to 2 minutes.* Sprinkle with powdered sugar and serve immediately with maple syrup and additional "M&M's"® Semi-Sweet Chocolate Mini Baking Bits. *Makes 4 Belgian waffles*

*Check the manufacturer's directions for recommended amount of batter and baking time.

Chocolate Waffles: Substitute 1¼ cups biscuit baking mix, ¼ cup unsweetened cocoa powder and ½ cup sugar for biscuit baking mix. Prepare and cook as directed above.

Tip: These waffles make a great dessert too! Serve them with a scoop of ice cream, chocolate sauce and a sprinkle of "M&M's"® Chocolate Mini Baking Bits.

Whip 'em Up Wacky Waffles

Banana Chocolate Chip Muffins

2 ripe, medium DOLE® Bananas
1 cup packed brown sugar
2 eggs
½ cup (1 stick) margarine, melted
1 teaspoon vanilla extract
2¼ cups all-purpose flour
2 teaspoons baking powder
½ teaspoon ground cinnamon
½ teaspoon salt
1 cup chocolate chips
½ cup chopped walnuts

• Purée bananas in blender; measure 1 cup for recipe. Beat bananas, sugar, eggs, margarine and vanilla in medium bowl until well blended.

• Combine flour, baking powder, cinnamon and salt in large bowl. Stir in chocolate chips and nuts. Make well in center of dry ingredients. Add banana mixture. Stir just until blended. Spoon into well greased 2½-inch muffin pan cups.

• Bake at 350°F 25 to 30 minutes or until toothpick inserted in centers comes out clean. Cool slightly; remove from pan and place on wire rack.

Makes 12 muffins

Prep Time: 20 minutes
Bake Time: 30 minutes

Lots o' Chocolate Bread

2 cups mini semisweet chocolate chips, divided
⅔ cup packed light brown sugar
½ cup (1 stick) butter, softened
2 eggs
2½ cups all-purpose flour
1½ cups applesauce
1½ teaspoons vanilla
1 teaspoon baking soda
1 teaspoon baking powder
½ teaspoon salt
1 tablespoon shortening (do not use butter, margarine, spread or oil)

1. Preheat oven to 350°F. Grease 5 (5½×3-inch) mini loaf pans. Place 1 cup chocolate chips in small microwavable bowl. Microwave on HIGH 1 minute; stir. Microwave at 30-second intervals, stirring after each interval, until chocolate is melted and smooth; set aside.

2. Beat brown sugar and butter in large bowl with electric mixer until creamy. Add melted chocolate and eggs; beat until well blended. Add flour, applesauce, vanilla, baking soda, baking powder and salt; beat until well blended. Stir in ½ cup chocolate chips. Spoon batter evenly into prepared pans.

3. Bake 35 to 40 minutes or until centers crack and are dry to the touch. Cool in pans on wire racks 10 minutes. Remove from pans; cool completely on wire racks.

4. Place remaining ½ cup chocolate chips and shortening in small microwavable bowl. Microwave on HIGH 1 minute; stir. Microwave at 30-second intervals, stirring after each interval, until chocolate is melted and mixture is smooth. Drizzle loaves with glaze; let stand until set.   *Makes 5 mini loaves*

Toll House® Crumbcake

Topping
⅓ cup packed brown sugar
1 tablespoon all-purpose flour
2 tablespoons butter or margarine, softened
½ cup chopped nuts
2 cups (12-ounce package) NESTLÉ® TOLL HOUSE® Semi-Sweet
 Chocolate Mini Morsels, *divided*

Cake
1¾ cups all-purpose flour
1 teaspoon baking powder
1 teaspoon baking soda
¼ teaspoon salt
¾ cup granulated sugar
½ cup (1 stick) butter or margarine, softened
1 teaspoon vanilla extract
3 large eggs
1 cup sour cream

PREHEAT oven to 350°F. Grease 13×9-inch baking pan.

For Topping
COMBINE brown sugar, flour and butter in small bowl with pastry blender or two knives until crumbly. Stir in nuts and *½ cup* morsels.

For Cake
COMBINE flour, baking powder, baking soda and salt in small bowl. Beat granulated sugar, butter and vanilla extract in large mixer bowl until creamy. Add eggs, one at a time, beating well after each addition. Gradually add flour mixture alternately with sour cream. Fold in *remaining 1½ cups* morsels. Spread into prepared baking pan; sprinkle with topping.

BAKE for 25 to 35 minutes or until wooden pick inserted in center comes out clean. Cool in pan on wire rack.   *Makes 12 servings*

Toll House® Crumbcake

Gooey Caramel and Chocolate Pecan Rolls

2 loaves (1 pound each) frozen white bread dough
1 jar (12 ounces) caramel ice cream topping
⅔ cup coarsely chopped pecans
1 cup semisweet chocolate chips, divided
4 tablespoons butter, divided

1. Thaw bread dough according to package directions.

2. Preheat oven to 375°F. Divide caramel topping evenly between 2 (9-inch) round cake pans; spread to cover bottom of pans. Sprinkle pecans evenly over caramel.

3. Microwave ⅔ cup chocolate chips and 2 tablespoons butter in medium microwavable bowl on HIGH 30 seconds; stir. Microwave at 20-second intervals, if necessary, stirring until smooth.

4. Roll one loaf bread dough on lightly floured surface into 12×8-inch rectangle. Spread half of chocolate mixture over dough. Beginning from long side, roll up jelly-roll style to form 12-inch log, pinching seam to seal. Cut into 12 (1-inch) slices; arrange, cut sides down, in one prepared pan. Repeat with remaining dough and chocolate mixture.

5. Cover; let rise in warm place until nearly doubled in bulk, about 1 hour. Uncover and bake 20 to 25 minutes. Immediately invert onto serving plates.

6. Melt remaining ⅓ cup chocolate chips and 2 tablespoons butter in microwave as directed in step 3. Drizzle over warm rolls.

Makes 2 dozen rolls

Gooey Caramel and Chocolate Pecan Rolls

Peanut Butter Mini Muffins

⅓ cup creamy peanut butter
¼ cup (½ stick) butter, softened
¼ cup granulated sugar
¼ cup firmly packed light brown sugar
1 large egg
¾ cup buttermilk
3 tablespoons vegetable oil
¾ teaspoon vanilla extract
1½ cups all-purpose flour
¾ teaspoon baking powder
½ teaspoon baking soda
½ teaspoon salt
1¼ cups "M&M's"® Milk Chocolate Mini Baking Bits, divided
    Chocolate Glaze (recipe follows)

Preheat oven to 350°F. Lightly grease 36 (1¾-inch) mini muffin cups or line
with paper or foil liners; set aside. In large bowl cream peanut butter, butter
and sugars until light and fluffy; beat in egg. Beat in buttermilk, oil and
vanilla. In medium bowl combine flour, baking powder, baking soda and
salt; gradually blend into creamed mixture. Divide batter evenly among
prepared muffin cups. Sprinkle batter evenly with ¾ cup "M&M's"® Milk
Chocolate Mini Baking Bits. Bake 15 to 17 minutes or until toothpick
inserted in centers comes out clean. Cool completely on wire racks. Prepare
Chocolate Glaze. Place glaze in resealable plastic sandwich bag; seal bag.
Cut tiny piece off one corner of bag (not more than ⅛ inch). Drizzle glaze
over muffins. Decorate with remaining ½ cup "M&M's"® Milk Chocolate
Mini Baking Bits; let glaze set. Store in tightly covered container.

Makes 3 dozen mini muffins

Chocolate Glaze: In top of double boiler over hot water melt 2 (1-ounce)
squares semi-sweet chocolate and 1 tablespoon butter. Stir until smooth;
let cool slightly.

White Chocolate Chunk Muffins

2½ cups all-purpose flour
1 cup packed light brown sugar
⅓ cup unsweetened cocoa powder
2 teaspoons baking soda
½ teaspoon salt
1⅓ cups buttermilk
¼ cup (½ stick) plus 2 tablespoons butter, melted
2 eggs, beaten
1½ teaspoons vanilla
1½ cups chopped white chocolate

1. Preheat oven to 400°F. Grease 12 large (3½-inch) muffin pan cups.

2. Combine flour, sugar, cocoa, baking soda and salt in large bowl. Combine buttermilk, butter, eggs and vanilla in small bowl until blended. Stir into flour mixture just until moistened. Fold in white chocolate. Spoon into prepared muffin cups, filling half full.

3. Bake 25 to 30 minutes or until toothpick inserted into centers comes out clean. Cool in pan on wire rack 5 minutes. Remove from pan; cool on wire rack 10 minutes. *Makes 12 large muffins*

Cocoa Nut Bundles

1 can (8 ounces) refrigerated quick crescent dinner rolls
2 tablespoons butter or margarine, softened
1 tablespoon granulated sugar
2 teaspoons HERSHEY'S Cocoa
¼ cup chopped nuts
   Powdered sugar (optional)

1. Heat oven to 375°F. Unroll dough on ungreased cookie sheet and separate to form 8 triangles.

2. Combine butter, granulated sugar and cocoa in small bowl. Add nuts; mix well. Divide chocolate mixture evenly among triangles, placing on wide end of triangle. Take dough on either side of mixture and pull up and over, tucking ends under. Continue rolling dough toward opposite point.

3. Bake 9 to 10 minutes or until golden brown. Sprinkle with powdered sugar, if desired; serve warm. *Makes 8 rolls*

White Chocolate Chunk Muffins

Peanut Butter Mini Chip Loaves

3 cups all-purpose flour
1½ teaspoons baking powder
1 teaspoon baking soda
1 teaspoon salt
1 cup creamy peanut butter
½ cup (1 stick) butter, softened
½ cup granulated sugar
½ cup packed light brown sugar
2 eggs
1½ cups buttermilk*
2 teaspoons vanilla
1 cup mini semisweet chocolate chips

Or, substitute soured fresh milk. To sour milk, place 1½ tablespoons lemon juice plus enough milk to equal 1½ cups in 2-cup measure. Stir; let stand 5 minutes before using.

1. Preheat oven to 350°F. Grease two 8½×4½-inch loaf pans. Sift flour, baking powder, baking soda and salt into large bowl; set aside.

2. Beat peanut butter, butter, granulated sugar and brown sugar in large bowl with electric mixer at medium speed until light and fluffy. Beat in eggs, one at a time; beat in buttermilk and vanilla.

3. Gradually add flour mixture, beating at low speed. Stir in chocolate chips. Spoon batter into prepared pans.

4. Bake 45 minutes or until toothpick inserted into centers comes out clean. Cool in pans on wire racks 10 minutes. Remove from pans; cool completely on wire racks. *Makes 2 loaves*

Peanut Butter Mini Chip Loaf

Acknowledgments

The publisher would like to thank the companies and organizations listed below for the use of their recipes and photographs in this publication.

ACH Food Companies, Inc.

Crisco is a registered trademark of The J.M. Smucker Company

Dole Food Company, Inc.

Domino® Foods, Inc.

Duncan Hines® and Moist Deluxe® are registered trademarks of Pinnacle Foods Corp.

EAGLE BRAND®

The Hershey Company

JOLLY TIME® Pop Corn

Keebler® Company

© Mars, Incorporated 2006

McIlhenny Company (TABASCO® brand Pepper Sauce)

Nestlé USA

The Quaker® Oatmeal Kitchens

Smucker's® trademark of The J.M. Smucker Company

Unilever Foods North America

Walnut Marketing Board

Watkins Incorporated

Index

A

Almonds
Almond Brownies, 42
Chocolate Almond Biscotti, 12
Chocolate Almond Frosting, 64
Chocolate Almond Macaroon Bars, 60
Chocolate Almond Torte, 62
Double Chocolate Banana Cookies, 27

B

Bananas
Banana Chocolate Chip Muffins, 142
Chocolate Banana Split Pie, 103
Double Chocolate Banana Cookies, 27
Frozen Chocolate-Covered Bananas, 124
Fudgy Banana Oat Cake, 71
Fudgy Banana Rocky Road Clusters, 122

Beverages
Canadian Cocoa, 128
Citrus Cocoa, 128
Cocoa Au Lait, 128
Creamy Hot Chocolate, 116
Hot Cocoa, 128
Mint Cocoa, 128
Quick Microwave Cocoa, 128
Spanish Chocolate, 122
Spiced Cocoa, 128
Swiss Cocoa, 128

Breads
Chocolate Chip Coffeecake, 136
Cocoa Nut Bundles, 150
Gooey Caramel and Chocolate Pecan Rolls, 146
Lots o' Chocolate Bread, 143
Peanut Butter Mini Chip Loaves, 152
Petit Pain au Chocolate, 134

Brownies
Almond Brownies, 42
Chunky Caramel Nut Brownies, 52
Easy Double Chocolate Chip Brownies, 46
Easy Fudgy Mayo Brownies, 48
Hershey's Best Brownies, 36
Mini Brownie Cups, 94
Buried Cherry Bars, 58

C

Cakes (*see also* **Cakes, Layer; Cakes, 13×9**)
Chocolate Intensity, 70
Chocolate Lava Cakes, 68
Chocolate Petits Fours, 96
Chocolate Sheet Cake, 76
Chocolate Squares with Nutty Caramel Sauce, 80
Dandy Cake, 84
Decadent Chocolate Lava Cake, 77
Glazed Chocolate Pound Cake, 82
Toll House® Crumbcake, 144

Cakes, Layer
Chocolate Almond Torte, 62
Chocolate Raspberry Cake, 65
Super-Moist Chocolate Layer Cake, 77
Yellow Mayonnaise Cake, 77

Cakes, 13×9
Fudgy Banana Oat Cake, 71
Hershey's Red Velvet Cake, 72
Hot Fudge Sundae Cake, 66
Pecan Coconut-Topped Cake, 77
Canadian Cocoa, 128

Candy
Chocolate Mint Truffles, 92
Chocolate Peanut Butter Chip Glazed Fudge, 114
Cookies and Cream Cheesecake Bonbons, 100
Cookies 'n' Crème Fudge, 106
Cracker Toffee, 90
Festive Fudge, 114
Fudgy Banana Rocky Road Clusters, 122
German Chocolate No-Cook Fudge, 118
Marshmallow Fudge, 114
No-Bake Chocolate Peanut Butter Balls, 129
Passion Truffles, 120
Raisin Clusters, 112
Rocky Road Candy, 120

Caramel
Chocolate Squares with Nutty Caramel Sauce, 80
Chunky Caramel Nut Brownies, 52
Gooey Caramel and Chocolate Pecan Rolls, 146

Index

Cheesecakes
Chocolate Chip Cheesecake Bars, 40
Mini Chocolate Cheesecakes, 78
Mini Swirl Cheesecakes, 78
Triple Chip Cheesecake, 74
Chewy Brownie Cookies, 26
Choco-Hot Sauce, 118
Chocolate Almond Biscotti, 12
Chocolate Almond Frosting, 64
Chocolate Almond Macaroon Bars, 60
Chocolate Almond Torte, 62
Chocolate Banana Split Pie, 103
Chocolate Chip Cheesecake Bars, 40
Chocolate Chip Coffeecake, 136
Chocolate Chip Macaroons, 10, 28
Chocolate Crackletops, 10
Chocolate Croissant Pudding, 100
Chocolate-Dipped Oat Drops, 13
Chocolate Gingersnaps, 4
Chocolate Glaze, 42, 148
Chocolate Intensity, 70
Chocolate Lava Cakes, 68
Chocolate Mint Truffles, 92
Chocolate Mudslide Frozen Pie, 88
Chocolate Nut Bars, 54
Chocolate Nut Topping, 136
Chocolate Peanut Butter Candy Bars, 110
Chocolate Peanut Butter Chip Cookies, 8
Chocolate Peanut Butter Chip Glazed Fudge, 114
Chocolate Peanut Butter Cups, 86
Chocolate Peanut Butter Pie, 117
Chocolate Peanutty Crumble Bars, 54
Chocolate-Pecan Angels, 18
Chocolate Petits Fours, 96
Chocolate Pistachio Cookies, 32
Chocolate Pudding, 104
Chocolate Raspberry Cake, 65
Chocolate Raspberry Crumb Bars, 38
Chocolate Sheet Cake, 76
Chocolate Squares with Nutty Caramel Sauce, 80
Chocolate Topping, 84
Chocolate Triple Layer Pie, 106
Chocolate Waffles, 140
Chocolate Walnut Meringues, 22
Choco-Peanut Butter-Brickle Cookies, 16
Chunky Caramel Nut Brownies, 52

Citrus Cocoa, 128
Cocoa Au Lait, 128
Cocoa Cappuccino Mousse, 98
Cocoa Nut Bundles, 150
Coconut
Chocolate Almond Macaroon Bars, 60
Chocolate Chip Macaroons, 10, 28
Chocolate-Dipped Oat Drops, 13
Double Chocolate Oat Drops, 13
Fudgey Coconut Clusters, 28
Magic Cookie Bars, 44
Magic Peanut Cookie Bars, 44
Magic Rainbow Cookie Bars, 44
Pecan Coconut-Topped Cake, 77
7-Layer Magic Cookie Bars, 44
Coffee
Chocolate Intensity, 70
Chocolate Mudslide Frozen Pie, 88
Cocoa Cappuccino Mousse, 98
Mocha Glaze, 94
Mocha-Macadamia Nut Muffins, 132
Rich Chocolate Mousse, 104
Spanish Chocolate, 122
Swiss Cocoa, 128
Cookies and Cream Cheesecake Bonbons, 100
Cookies 'n' Crème Fudge, 106
Cookies, Bar
Buried Cherry Bars, 58
Chocolate Almond Macaroon Bars, 60
Chocolate Chip Cheesecake Bars, 40
Chocolate Nut Bars, 54
Chocolate Peanut Butter Candy Bars, 110
Chocolate Peanutty Crumble Bars, 54
Chocolate Raspberry Crumb Bars, 38
Crispy Cocoa Bars, 36
Heavenly Oat Bars, 49
Magic Cookie Bars, 44
Magic Peanut Cookie Bars, 44
Magic Rainbow Cookie Bars, 44
Marshmallow Krispie Bars, 48
Marvelous Cookie Bars, 50
No-Bake Chocolate Peanut Butter Bars, 56
Nutty Chocolate Chunk Bars, 46
Peanut Butter Fudge Brownie Bars, 41

Cookies, Bar *(continued)*
Pop Corn S'Mores, 56
7-Layer Magic Cookie Bars, 44
White Chocolate Squares, 34
Cookies, Drop
Chewy Brownie Cookies, 26
Chocolate Chip Macaroons, 10, 28
Chocolate-Dipped Oat Drops, 13
Chocolate-Pecan Angels, 18
Chocolate Pistachio Cookies, 32
Chocolate Walnut Meringues, 22
Choco-Peanut Butter-Brickle
Cookies, 16
Double Chocolate Banana Cookies,
27
Double Chocolate Oat Drops, 13
Fudgey Coconut Clusters, 28
Hershey's "Perfectly Chocolate"
Chocolate Chip Cookies, 24
Jumbo 3-Chip Cookies, 6
Malted Milk Cookies, 8
Milk Chocolate Florentine Cookies,
20
Moon Rocks, 18
No-Bake Peanutty Chocolate Drops,
30
Quick Chocolate Softies, 22
Super Chocolate Cookies, 14
Cookies, Shaped
Chocolate Almond Biscotti, 12
Chocolate Crackletops, 10
Chocolate Gingersnaps, 4
Chocolate Peanut Butter Chip
Cookies, 8
Devil's Food Fudge Cookies, 30
Cracker Toffee, 90
Creamy Hot Chocolate, 116
Crispy Cocoa Bars, 36

D
Dandy Cake, 84
Decadent Chocolate Lava Cake, 77
Devil's Food Fudge Cookies, 30
Dips and Sauces
Choco-Hot Sauce, 118
Hot Fudge Sauce, 123
Peanutty Chocolate Sauce, 126
Special Dark® Fudge Fondue, 126
Ultimate Chocolate Dip, 117
Double Chocolate Banana Cookies, 27
Double Chocolate Oat Drops, 13

Double Chocolate Zucchini Muffins,
137

E
Easy Double Chocolate Chip Brownies,
46
Easy Fudgy Mayo Brownies, 48
Easy Homemade Chocolate Ice Cream,
90

F
Festive Fudge, 114
Frostings and Glazes
Chocolate Almond Frosting, 64
Chocolate Glaze, 42, 148
Chocolate Topping, 84
Mocha Glaze, 94
Frozen Chocolate-Covered Bananas,
124
Frozen Desserts
Chocolate Mudslide Frozen Pie, 88
Chocolate Peanut Butter Pie, 117
Easy Homemade Chocolate Ice
Cream, 90
Frozen Chocolate-Covered Bananas,
124
Fruit *(see also individual listings)*
Buried Cherry Bars, 58
Chocolate Raspberry Cake, 65
Chocolate Raspberry Crumb Bars, 38
Luscious Chocolate-Covered
Strawberries, 124
Fudgey Chocolate Chip Muffins, 138
Fudgey Coconut Clusters, 28
Fudgey Peanut Butter Chip Muffins, 138
Fudgy Banana Oat Cake, 71
Fudgy Banana Rocky Road Clusters,
122

G
German Chocolate No-Cook Fudge,
118
Glazed Chocolate Pound Cake, 82
Gooey Caramel and Chocolate Pecan
Rolls, 146

H
Heavenly Chocolate Mousse Pie, 98
Heavenly Oat Bars, 49
Hershey's "Perfectly Chocolate"
Chocolate Chip Cookies, 24

Hershey₀s Best Brownies, 36
Hershey₀s Red Velvet Cake, 72
Hot Cocoa, 128
Hot Fudge Sauce, 123
Hot Fudge Sundae Cake, 66

J
Jumbo 3-Chip Cookies, 6

L
Lots o' Chocolate Bread, 143
Luscious Chocolate-Covered
    Strawberries, 124

M
Magic Cookie Bars, 44
Magic Peanut Cookie Bars, 44
Magic Rainbow Cookie Bars, 44
Malted Milk Cookies, 8
Marshmallows
    Crispy Cocoa Bars, 36
    Fudgy Banana Rocky Road Clusters,
        122
    Marshmallow Fudge, 114
    Marshmallow Krispie Bars, 48
    Pop Corn S'Mores, 56
    Rocky Road Candy, 120
Marvelous Cookie Bars, 50
Milk Chocolate Florentine Cookies, 20
Milk Chocolate Pots de Crème, 116
Mini Brownie Cups, 94
Mini Chocolate Cheesecakes, 78
Mini Chocolate Pies, 112
Mini Swirl Cheesecakes, 78
Mint Cocoa, 128
Mocha Glaze, 94
Mocha-Macadamia Nut Muffins, 132
Moon Rocks, 18
Mousse
    Cocoa Cappuccino Mousse, 98
    Heavenly Chocolate Mousse Pie, 98
    Quick Chocolate Mousse, 129
    Rich Chocolate Mousse, 104
    White Chocolate Mousse, 102
Muffins
    Banana Chocolate Chip Muffins, 142
    Double Chocolate Zucchini Muffins,
        137
    Fudgey Chocolate Chip Muffins, 138
    Fudgey Peanut Butter Chip Muffins,
        138

Muffins *(continued)*
    Mocha-Macadamia Nut Muffins, 132
    Peanut Butter Mini Muffins, 148
    White Chocolate Chunk Muffins, 150

N
Nestlé® Toll House® Chocolate Chip
    Pie, 108
No-Bake Chocolate Peanut Butter
    Balls, 129
No-Bake Chocolate Peanut Butter
    Bars, 56
No-Bake Peanutty Chocolate Drops, 30
Nuts *(see also individual listings)*
    Chocolate Nut Bars, 54
    Chocolate Pistachio Cookies, 32
    Chocolate Sheet Cake, 76
    Cocoa Nut Bundles, 150
    Jumbo 3-Chip Cookies, 6
    Magic Cookie Bars, 44
    Mocha-Macadamia Nut Muffins, 132
    Nestlé® Toll House® Chocolate Chip
        Pie, 108
Nutty Chocolate Chunk Bars, 46

O
Oats
    Chocolate-Dipped Oat Drops, 13
    Double Chocolate Banana Cookies,
        27
    Double Chocolate Oat Drops, 13
    Fudgy Banana Oat Cake, 71
    Heavenly Oat Bars, 49
    Marvelous Cookie Bars, 50
    Milk Chocolate Florentine Cookies,
        20
    Moon Rocks, 18
    No-Bake Peanutty Chocolate Drops,
        30
    Nutty Chocolate Chunk Bars, 46

P
Passion Truffles, 120
Peanut Butter
    Chocolate Peanut Butter Candy Bars,
        110
    Chocolate Peanut Butter Chip
        Cookies, 8
    Chocolate Peanut Butter Chip Glazed
        Fudge, 114
    Chocolate Peanut Butter Cups, 86

Peanut Butter *(continued)*
Chocolate Peanut Butter Pie, 117
Choco-Peanut Butter-Brickle
Cookies, 16
Fudgey Peanut Butter Chip Muffins,
138
Marshmallow Krispie Bars, 48
No-Bake Chocolate Peanut Butter
Balls, 129
No-Bake Chocolate Peanut Butter
Bars, 56
Nutty Chocolate Chunk Bars, 46
Peanut Butter Fudge Brownie Bars,
41
Peanut Butter Mini Chip Loaves, 152
Peanut Butter Mini Muffins, 148
Peanutty Chocolate Sauce, 126
Two Great Tastes Pudding Parfaits,
102
Peanuts
Fudgy Banana Rocky Road Clusters,
122
Magic Peanut Cookie Bars, 44
No-Bake Peanutty Chocolate Drops,
30
Nutty Chocolate Chunk Bars, 46
Rocky Road Candy, 120
Pecans
Chocolate Nut Topping, 136
Chocolate-Pecan Angels, 18
Chocolate Squares with Nutty
Caramel Sauce, 80
Chunky Caramel Nut Brownies, 52
Cracker Toffee, 90
German Chocolate No-Cook Fudge,
118
Gooey Caramel and Chocolate Pecan
Rolls, 146
Peanut Butter Fudge Brownie Bars, 41
Pecan Coconut-Topped Cake, 77
White Chocolate Squares, 34
Petit Pain au Chocolate, 134
Pies
Chocolate Banana Split Pie, 103
Chocolate Mudslide Frozen Pie, 88
Chocolate Peanut Butter Pie, 117
Chocolate Triple Layer Pie, 106
Heavenly Chocolate Mousse Pie, 98
Mini Chocolate Pies, 112
Nestlé® Toll House® Chocolate Chip
Pie, 108

Pop Corn S'Mores, 56

Q
Quick Chocolate Mousse, 129
Quick Chocolate Softies, 22
Quick Microwave Cocoa, 128

R
Raisin Clusters, 112
Rich Chocolate Mousse, 104
Rocky Road Candy, 120

S
7-Layer Magic Cookie Bars, 44
Spanish Chocolate, 122
Special Dark® Fudge Fondue, 126
Spiced Cocoa, 128
Super Chocolate Cookies, 14
Super-Moist Chocolate Layer Cake,
77
Swiss Cocoa, 128

T
Toll House® Crumbcake, 144
Toll House® Mini Morsel Pancakes,
130
Triple Chip Cheesecake, 74
Two Great Tastes Pudding Parfaits,
102

U
Ultimate Chocolate Dip, 117

W
Walnuts
Chocolate-Dipped Oat Drops, 13
Chocolate Mint Truffles, 92
Chocolate Walnut Meringues, 22
Double Chocolate Oat Drops, 13
Whip 'em Up Wacky Waffles, 140
White Chocolate
Cookies 'n' Crème Fudge, 106
Quick Chocolate Softies, 22
Triple Chip Cheesecake, 74
White Chocolate Chunk Muffins,
150
White Chocolate Mousse, 102
White Chocolate Squares, 34

Y
Yellow Mayonnaise Cake, 77

Metric Chart

VOLUME MEASUREMENTS (dry)

$1/8$ teaspoon = 0.5 mL
$1/4$ teaspoon = 1 mL
$1/2$ teaspoon = 2 mL
$3/4$ teaspoon = 4 mL
1 teaspoon = 5 mL
1 tablespoon = 15 mL
2 tablespoons = 30 mL
$1/4$ cup = 60 mL
$1/3$ cup = 75 mL
$1/2$ cup = 125 mL
$2/3$ cup = 150 mL
$3/4$ cup = 175 mL
1 cup = 250 mL
2 cups = 1 pint = 500 mL
3 cups = 750 mL
4 cups = 1 quart = 1 L

VOLUME MEASUREMENTS (fluid)

1 fluid ounce (2 tablespoons) = 30 mL
4 fluid ounces ($1/2$ cup) = 125 mL
8 fluid ounces (1 cup) = 250 mL
12 fluid ounces ($1 1/2$ cups) = 375 mL
16 fluid ounces (2 cups) = 500 mL

WEIGHTS (mass)

$1/2$ ounce = 15 g
1 ounce = 30 g
3 ounces = 90 g
4 ounces = 120 g
8 ounces = 225 g
10 ounces = 285 g
12 ounces = 360 g
16 ounces = 1 pound = 450 g

DIMENSIONS

$1/16$ inch = 2 mm
$1/8$ inch = 3 mm
$1/4$ inch = 6 mm
$1/2$ inch = 1.5 cm
$3/4$ inch = 2 cm
1 inch = 2.5 cm

OVEN TEMPERATURES

250°F = 120°C
275°F = 140°C
300°F = 150°C
325°F = 160°C
350°F = 180°C
375°F = 190°C
400°F = 200°C
425°F = 220°C
450°F = 230°C

BAKING PAN SIZES

Utensil	Size in Inches/Quarts	Metric Volume	Size in Centimeters
Baking or	$8 \times 8 \times 2$	2 L	$20 \times 20 \times 5$
Cake Pan	$9 \times 9 \times 2$	2.5 L	$23 \times 23 \times 5$
(square or	$12 \times 8 \times 2$	3 L	$30 \times 20 \times 5$
rectangular)	$13 \times 9 \times 2$	3.5 L	$33 \times 23 \times 5$
Loaf Pan	$8 \times 4 \times 3$	1.5 L	$20 \times 10 \times 7$
	$9 \times 5 \times 3$	2 L	$23 \times 13 \times 7$
Round Layer	$8 \times 1 1/2$	1.2 L	20×4
Cake Pan	$9 \times 1 1/2$	1.5 L	23×4
Pie Plate	$8 \times 1 1/4$	750 mL	20×3
	$9 \times 1 1/4$	1 L	23×3
Baking Dish	1 quart	1 L	—
or Casserole	$1 1/2$ quart	1.5 L	—
	2 quart	2 L	—